Pro Bash Programming

Scripting the GNU/Linux Shell

Chris F.A. Johnson

Apress®

Pro Bash Programming: Scripting the GNU/Linux Shell

ISBN-13 (pbk): 978-1-4302-1997-2

ISBN-13 (electronic): 978-1-4302-1998-9

Printed and bound in the United States of America 9 8 7 6 5 4 3 2 1

Distributed to the book trade worldwide by Springer-Verlag New York, Inc., 233 Spring Street, 6th Floor, New York, NY 10013. Phone 1-800-SPRINGER, fax 201-348-4505, e-mail orders-ny@springer-sbm.com, or visit http://www.springeronline.com.

For information on translations, please contact Apress directly at 233 Spring Street, New York, NY 10013. E-mail info@apress.com, or visit http://www.apress.com.

Apress and friends of ED books may be purchased in bulk for academic, corporate, or promotional use. eBook versions and licenses are also available for most titles. For more information, reference our Special Bulk Sales–eBook Licensing web page at http://www.apress.com/info/bulksales.

The source code for this book is available to readers at http://www.apress.com.

Contents at a Glance

Contents

About the Author

■After almost 20 years in magazine and newspaper publishing, variously as writer, editor, graphic designer, and production manager, **Chris F.A. Johnson** now earns his living composing cryptic crossword puzzles, teaching chess, designing and coding web sites, and programming...and writing books about shell scripting. His first book, *Shell Scripting Recipes: A Problem-Solution Approach*, was published by Apress in 2005.

Introduced to Unix in 1990, Chris learned shell scripting because there was no C compiler on the system. His first major project was a menu-driven, user-extensible database system with a report generator. Constantly writing scripts for any and all purposes, his recent shell projects have included utilities for manipulating crossword puzzles and preparing chess resources for his students.

About the Technical Reviewer

 **Ed Schaefer** is an ex-paratrooper, an ex-military intelligence officer, an ex-oil field service engineer, and a past contributing editor and columnist for *Sys Admin*. He's not a total has-been. He earned a BSEE from South Dakota School of Mines and an MBA from USD.

Currently, he fixes microstrategy and teradata problems—with an occasional foray into Linux—for a Fortune 50 company.

Introduction

Although most users think of the shell as an interactive command interpreter, it is really a programming language in which each statement runs a command. Because it must satisfy both the interactive and programming aspects of command execution, it is a strange language, shaped as much by history as by design.

Brian Kernighan and Rob Pike, *The UNIX Programming Environment*, Prentice-Hall, 1984

The shell *is* a programming language. Don't let anyone tell you otherwise. The shell is not just glue that sticks bits together. The shell is a lot more than a tool that runs other tools. *The shell is a complete programming language!*

When a Linux user asked me about membership databases, I asked him what he really needed. He wanted to store names and addresses for a couple of hundred members and print mailing labels for each of them. I recommended using a text editor to store the information in a text file, and I provided a shell script to create the labels in PostScript. (The script, ps-labels, appeared in my first book, *Shell Scripting Recipes: A Problem-Solution Approach*.)

When the SWEN worm was dumping hundreds of megabytes of junk into my mailbox every few minutes, I wrote a shell script to filter them out on the mail server and download the remaining mail to my home computer. That script has been doing its job for several years.

I used to tell people that I did most of my programming in the shell but switched to C for anything that needed the extra speed. It has been several years since I have needed to use C, so I no longer mention it. I do everything in the shell.

A shell script is as much a program as anything written in C, Python, or any other language. Just because shell scripts are easier to write doesn't mean they should take a backseat to compiled programs or other scripting languages. I use the terms *script* and *program* interchangeably when referring to tasks written in the shell.

Why the Shell?

Some Linux users do all of their work in a GUI environment and never see a command line. Most, however, use the shell at least occasionally and know something about Unix commands. It's not a big step from there to saving oft-repeated commands in a script file. When they need to extend the capabilities of their system, the shell is the natural way to go.

The shell also has important advantages over other programming languages:

- It interfaces simply and seamlessly with the hundreds of Unix utilities.
- It automatically expands wildcards into a list of file names.
- Lists contained in a variable are automatically split into their constituent parts.

Just the Shell, Ma'am, Just the Shell

While most shell programs *do* call external utilities, a lot of programming can be done entirely in the shell. Many scripts call just one or two utilities for information that is used later in the script. Some scripts are little more than wrappers for other commands such as awk, grep, or sed.

This book is about programming in the shell itself. There's a sprinkling of the second type, where the script gets information (such as the current date and time) and then processes it. The third type gets barely more than a cursory nod.

A Brief History of sh

The Bourne shell was the first Unix shell in general use. It was much more limited than today's shells, so it *was* primarily a tool to run other tools. It had variables, loops, and conditional execution, but the real work was done almost entirely by external utilities.

The C shell, csh, added command history, arithmetic, and other features that made it popular as a command-line interpreter, but it was not suitable for more than trivial scripts.

The KornShell, developed by David Korn at AT&T Bell Labs, combined the Bourne shell syntax with features of the C shell. It was compatible with the Bourne shell, bringing important functionality into the shell itself and making script execution much faster. Until the year 2000, when it was opened up, ksh was proprietary, closed-source software.

The GNU Project, needing a free, open-source shell, introduced bash. Like all modern shells, bash is a POSIX shell. It also has many added enhancements.

Which Version of Bash?

This book is aimed at users of bash-3 and later, but much of the book will work with bash-2.05. Features introduced in bash-4.0, are covered, but it is noted that they are newer additions. Wherever possible without loss of efficiency, the scripts in this book are written to run in any POSIX shell. It is often noted when a statement in a script is nonstandard or uses bash syntax. That means that it is not POSIX compliant. Most functions, however, will not run in a POSIX shell because they almost always use the local builtin command.

Some Linux distributions modify their versions of bash: Debian removes network socket capabilities. Mandriva removes the builtin time command. For this reason, I recommend compiling your own copy of bash. The source code is available from http://tiswww.case.edu/php/chet/bash/bashtop.html, and it compiles without trouble almost anywhere.

Who Will Benefit from This Book?

If you're an experienced shell programmer, this book will provide insight into the arcana of shell scripting, helping you write more, and more efficient, scripts.

If you have dabbled in shell scripting, I hope this book will encourage you to experiment further.

If you are new to shell scripting, this book will get you started and help you quickly become a proficient shell programmer.

No matter what your level of experience, this book will enable you to program tasks that aren't already dealt with on your system.

What's in the Book?

From writing your first program to using the mouse in your scripts, this book runs the gamut from simple to complex and from the obvious to the obscure. It covers every technique you will need to write efficient shell programs.

Chapter 1, Hello, World! Your First Shell Program, presents the traditional first program in any language. It prints "Hello, World!" The chapter discusses how to write the script, what to name it, and where to put it.

Chapter 2, Input, Output, and Throughput, demonstrates output using the echo and printf commands and introduces the read command for input. It also examines redirecting both input and output and connecting commands with pipelines.

Chapter 3, Looping and Branching, explains the looping statements, for, while, and until; the branching statement if; and the conditional operators && and ||.

Chapter 4, Command-Line Parsing and Expansion, describes how the shell parses a command line, from word splitting to parameter expansion.

Chapter 5, Variables and Parameters, covers all the possibilities of parameters and variables, from scalar variables to associative arrays and from default substitution to search and replace.

Chapter 6, Shell Functions, delves into the syntax of function definitions and defines a number of useful routines.

Chapter 7, String Manipulation, contains a number of functions for dicing and splicing strings.

Chapter 8, File Operations and Commands, uses more external commands than the rest of the book put together. That's because looping through a large file with the shell is painfully slow, and the Unix utilities are very efficient. This chapter also tells you when not to use those utilities.

Chapter 9, Reserved Words and Builtin Commands, looks at a number of commands that are built into the shell itself.

Chapter 10, Writing Bug-Free Scripts and Debugging the Rest, takes a buggy script and takes you step-by-step through fixing it, as well as showing you how to prevent bugs in the first place.

Chapter 11, Programming for the Command Line, is for those people who spend a lot of time at the command prompt. These programs and functions reduce the typing to a minimum.

Chapter 12, Runtime configuration, describes seven methods of altering a program's runtime behavior.

Chapter 13, Data Processing, deals with manipulating different types of data in the shell.

Chapter 14, Scripting the Screen, shows you how to write to the screen as if it were a canvas rather than a teletypewriter.

Chapter 15, Entry-Level Programming, presents techniques for getting input from a user, both using single keypresses and entering and editing a line of text. It concludes with routines for using the mouse in shell scripts.

The **appendix** lists all the variables used by bash with a description of each.

Downloading the Code

The source code for this book is available to readers as a gzipped tarball file at www.apress.com in the Downloads section of this book's home page. Please feel free to visit the Apress web site and download all the code there. You can also check for errata and find related titles from Apress.

Contacting the Author

The author maintains a web site at http://cfajohnson.com/ and can be reached via e-mail at shell@cfajohnson.com.

## CHAPTER 1

Hello, World!
Your First Shell Program

A *shell script* is a file containing one or more commands that you would type on the command line. This chapter describes how to create such a file and make it executable. It also covers some other issues surrounding shell scripts, including what to name the files, where to put them, and how to run them.

I will begin with the first program traditionally demonstrated in every computer language: a program that prints "Hello, World!" in your terminal. It's a simple program, but it is enough to demonstrate a number of important concepts. The code itself is the simplest part of this chapter. Naming the file and deciding where to put it are not complicated tasks, but they are important.

For most of this chapter, you will be working in a terminal. it could be a virtual terminal, a terminal window, or even a dumb terminal. In your terminal, the shell will immediately execute any commands you type (after you press Enter, of course).

You should be in your home directory, which you can find in the variable $HOME:

```
echo $HOME
```

You can find the current directory with either the pwd command or the PWD variable:

```
pwd
echo "$PWD"
```

If you are not in your home directory, you can get there by typing cd and pressing Enter at the shell prompt.

The Code

The code is nothing more than this:

```
echo Hello, World!
```

There are three words on this command line: the command itself and two arguments. The command, echo, prints its arguments separated by a single space and terminated with a newline.

The File

Before you turn that code into a script, you need to make two decisions: what you will call the file and where you will put it. The name should be unique (that is, it should not conflict with any other commands), and you should put it where the shell can find it.

The Naming of Scripts

Beginners often make the mistake of calling a trial script test. To see why that is bad, enter the following at the command prompt:

```
type test
```

The type command tells you what the shell will execute (and where it can be found if it is an external file) for any given command. In bash, type -a test will display all the commands that match the name test:

```
$ type test
test is a shell builtin
$ type -a test
test is a shell builtin
test is /usr/bin/test
```

As you can see, a command called test already exists; it is used to test file types and to compare values. If you call your script test, it will not be run when you type test at the shell prompt; the first command identified by type will be run instead. (I'll talk more about both type and test in later chapters.)

Typically, Unix command names are as short as possible. They are often the first two consonants of a descriptive word (for example, mv for **move** or ls for **list**) or the first letters of a descriptive phrase (for example , ps for **process status** or sed for **stream editor**).

For this exercise, call the script hw. Many shell programmers add a suffix, such as .sh, to indicate that the program is a shell script. The script doesn't need it, and I use one only for programs that are being developed. My suffix is -sh, and when the program is finished, I remove it. A shell script becomes another command and doesn't need to be distinguished from any other type of command.

Selecting a Directory for the Script

When the shell is given the name of a command to execute, it looks for that name in the directories listed in the PATH variable. This variable contains a colon-separated list of directories that contain executable commands. This is a typical value for $PATH:

```
/bin:/usr/bin:/usr/local/bin:/usr/games
```

If your program is not in one of the PATH directories, you must give a pathname, either absolute or relative, for bash to find it. An *absolute* pathname gives the location from the root of the filesystem, such as /home/chris/bin/hw; a *relative* pathname is given in relation to the current working directory (which should currently be your home directory), as in bin/hw.

Commands are usually stored in directories named `bin`, and a user's personal programs are stored in a `bin` subdirectory in the `$HOME` directory. To create that directory, use this command:

```
mkdir bin
```

Now that it exists, it must be added to the `PATH` variable:

```
PATH=$PATH:$HOME/bin
```

For this change to be applied to every shell you open, add it to a file that the shell will *source* when it is invoked. This will be `.bash_profile`, `.bashrc`, or `.profile` depending on how `bash` is invoked. These files are sourced only for interactive shells, not for scripts.

Creating the File and Running the Script

Usually you would use a text editor to create your program, but for a simple script like this, it's not necessary to call up an editor. You can create the file from the command line using redirection:

```
echo echo Hello, World! > bin/hw
```

The greater-than sign (>) tells the shell to send the output of a command to the specified file, rather than to the terminal. You'll learn more about redirection in Chapter 2.

The program can now be run by calling it as an argument to the shell command:

```
bash bin/hw
```

That works, but it's not entirely satisfactory. You want to be able to type `hw`, without having to precede it with `bash`, and have the command executed. To do that, give the file execute permissions:

```
chmod +x bin/hw
```

Now the command can be run using just its name:

```
$ hw
Hello, World!
```

Choosing and Using a Text Editor

For many people, one of the most important pieces of computer software is a word processor. Although I am using one to write this book (OpenOffice.org Writer), it's not something I use often. The last time I used a word processor was four years ago when I wrote my previous book. A text editor, on the other hand, is an indispensable tool. I use one for writing e-mail, Usenet articles, shell scripts, PostScript programs, web pages, and more.

A text editor operates on plain-text files. It stores only the characters you type; it doesn't add any hidden formatting codes. If I type A and press Enter in a text editor and save it, the file will contain exactly two characters: *A* and a newline. A word-processor file containing the same text would be thousands of times larger. (With *abiword*, the file contains 2,526 bytes; the OpenOffice.org file contains 8,192 bytes.)

You can write scripts in any text editor, from the basic e3 or nano to the full-featured emacs or nedit. The better text editors allow you to have more than one file open at a time. They make editing code easier with, for example, syntax highlighting, automatic indentation, autocompletion, spell checking, macros, search and replace, and undo. Ultimately, which editor you choose is a matter of personal preference. I use GNU emacs (see Figure 1-1).

■ **Note** In Windows text files, lines end with two characters: a *carriage return* (CR) and a *linefeed* (LF). On Unix systems, such as Linux, lines end with a single linefeed. If you write your programs in a Windows text editor, you must either save your files with Unix line endings or remove the carriage returns afterward.

```
□ parseopts-sh                                                            ×
Filesets File Edit Options Buffers Tools Insert Help
   #@ Demonstration of parsing options in a script
   progname=${0##*/}

   ## Default values
   verbose=0
   filename=

   optstring=f:v

   ## Keep calling getopts until there are no more options on the command line
   while getopts $optstring opt
   do
     case $opt in
       f) filename=$OPTARG ;;
       v) verbose=$(( $verbose + 1 )) ;;
       *) exit 3 ;;
     esac
   done

   ## Remove options from the command line
   ## $OPTIND points to the next, unparsed argument█
   shift $(( $OPTIND - 1 ))

   ## Check whether a filename was entered
   if [ -n "$filename" ]
   then
      if [ $verbose -gt 0 ]
      then
         printf "Filename is %s\n" "$filename"
      fi
   else
--:-- parseopts-sh   1% (22,48)   (Shell-script[bash] 1k/4G)-----------------------------
   Wrote /home/chris/public_html/BashProgramming/scr/parseopts-sh
```

Figure 1-1. Shell code in the GNU emacs text editor

Building a Better "Hello, World!"

Earlier in the chapter you created a script using redirection. That script was, to say the least, minimalist. All programs, even a one-liner, require documentation. Information should include at least the author, the date, and a description of the command. Open the file bin/hw in your text editor, and add the information in Listing 1-1 using *comments*.

Listing 1-1. hw

```
#!/bin/bash
#: Title      : hw
#: Date       : 2008-11-26
#: Author     : "Chris F.A. Johnson" <shell@cfajohnson.com>
#: Version    : 1.0
#: Description : print Hello, World!
#: Options    : None

printf "%s\n" "Hello, World!"
```

Comments begin with an octothorpe, or *hash* (#), at the beginning of a *word* and continue until the end of the line. The shell ignores them. I often add a character after the hash to indicate the type of comment. I can then search the file for the type I want, ignoring other comments.

The first line is a special type of comment called a *shebang* or *hash-bang*. It tells the system which *interpreter* to use to execute the file. The characters #! must appear at the very beginning of the first line; in other words, they must be the first two bytes of the file for it to be recognized.

Summary

The following are the commands, concepts, and variables you learned in this chapter.

Commands

- pwd: Prints the name of the current working directory

- cd: Changes the shell's working directory

- echo: Prints arguments separated by a space and terminated by a newline

- type: Displays information about a command

- mkdir: Creates a new directory

- chmod: Modifies the permissions of a file

- source: a.k.a. . (dot): executes a script in the current shell environment

- printf: Prints the arguments as specified by a format string

Concepts

- *Script*: This is a file containing commands to be executed by the shell.

- *Word*: A word is a sequence of characters considered to be a single unit by the shell.

- *Output redirection*: You can send the output of a command to a file rather than the terminal using `> FILENAME`.

- *Variables*: These are entities that store values.

- *Comments*: These consist of an unquoted *word* beginning with #. All remaining characters on that line constitute a comment and will be ignored.

- *Shebang or hash-bang*: This is a hash and an exclamation mark (#!) followed by the path to the interpreter that should execute the file.

- *Interpreter*: This is a program that reads a file and executes the statements it contains. It may be a shell or another language interpreter such as `awk` or `python`.

Variables

- `PWD` contains the pathname of the shell's current working directory.

- `HOME` stores the pathname of the user's home directory.

- `PATH` is a colon-separated list of directories in which command files are stored. The shell searches these directories for commands it is asked to execute.

Exercises

1. Write a script that creates a directory called `bpl` inside `$HOME`. Populate this directory with two subdirectories, `bin` and `scripts`.

2. Write a script to create the "Hello, World!" script, `hw`, in `$HOME/bpl/bin/`; make it executable; and then execute it.

CHAPTER 2

■ ■ ■

Input, Output, and Throughput

Two of the commands we used in Chapter 1 are workhorses of the shell scripter's stable: echo and printf. Both are bash *builtin* commands. Both print information to the *standard output* stream, but printf is much more powerful, and echo has its problems.

In this chapter, I'll cover echo and its problems, the capabilities of printf, the read command, and the standard input and output streams. I'll start, however, with an overview of parameters and variables.

Parameter and Variables

To quote the bash manual (type man bash at the command prompt to read it), "A parameter is an entity that stores values." There are three types of parameters: positional parameters, special parameters, and variables. *Positional parameters* are arguments present on the command line, and they are referenced by number. *Special parameters* are set by the shell to store information about aspects of its current state, such as the number of arguments and the exit code of the last command. Their names are nonalphanumeric characters (for example, *, #, and _). *Variables* are identified by a *name*. What's in a name? I'll explain that in the "Variables" section.

The value of a parameter is accessed by preceding its name, number, or character with a dollar sign, as in $3, $#, or $HOME. The name may be surrounded by braces, as in ${10}, ${PWD}, or ${USER}.

Positional Parameters

The arguments on the command line are available to a shell program as numbered parameters. The first argument is $1, the second is $2, and so on.

You can make the hw script from Chapter 1 more flexible by using a positional parameter. Listing 2-1 calls it hello.

Listing 2-1. hello

```
#: Description: print Hello and the first command-line argument
printf "Hello, %s!\n" "$1"
```

Now you can call the script with an argument to change its output:

```
$ hello John
Hello, John!
$ hello Susan
Hello, Susan!
```

The Bourne shell could only address up to nine positional parameters. If a script used $10, it would be interpreted as $1 followed by a zero. To be able to run old scripts, bash maintains that behavior. To access positional parameters greater than 9, the number must be enclosed in braces: ${15}.

Special *@#0$?_!- Parameters

The first two special parameters, $* and $@, expand to the value of all the positional parameters combined. $# expands to the number of positional parameters. $0 contains the path to the currently running script or to the shell itself if no script is being executed.

$$ contains the process identification number (PID) of the current process, $? is set to the exit code of the last-executed command, and $_ is set to the last argument to that command. $! contains the PID of the last command executed in the background, and $- is set to the option flags currently in effect.

I'll discuss these parameters in more detail as they come up in the course of writing scripts.

Variables

A *variable* is a parameter denoted by a name; a *name* is a word containing only letters, numbers, or underscores and beginning with a letter or an underscore.

Values can be assigned to variables in the following form:

```
name=VALUE
```

Many variables are set by the shell itself, including three you have already seen: HOME, PWD, and PATH. With only two minor exceptions, auto_resume and histchars, all the variables set by the shell are all uppercase letters.

Arguments and Options

The words entered after the command are its *arguments*. These are words separated by whitespace (one or more spaces or tabs). If the whitespace is escaped or quoted, it no longer separates words but becomes part of the word.

The following command lines all have four arguments:

```
echo 1 '2   3'   4 5
echo -n Now\ is  the  time
printf "%s %s\n" one two three
```

In the first line, the spaces between 2 and 3 are *quoted* because they are surrounded by single quotation marks. In the second, the space after now is escaped by a backslash, which is the shell's escape character.

In the final line, a space is quoted with double quotes.

In the second command, the first argument is an option. Traditionally, options to Unix commands are a single letter preceded by a hyphen, sometimes followed by an argument. The GNU commands found in Linux distributions often accept *long options* as well. These are words preceded by a double hyphen. For example, most GNU utilities have an option called --version that prints the version:

```
$ bash --version
GNU bash, version 4.0.10(1)-release (i686-pc-linux-gnuoldld)
Copyright (C) 2009 Free Software Foundation, Inc.
License GPLv3+: GNU GPL version 3 or later <http://gnu.org/licenses/gpl.html>

This is free software; you are free to change and redistribute it.
There is NO WARRANTY, to the extent permitted by law.
```

echo, and Why You Should Avoid It

When I started writing shell scripts, I soon learned about the two main branches of Unix: AT&T's System V and BSD. One of their differences was the behavior of echo. Built into all modern shells, echo prints its arguments with a single space between them to the standard output stream, followed by a newline:

```
$ echo The    quick  brown   fox
The quick brown fox
```

The default newline can be suppressed in one of two ways, depending on the shell:

```
$ echo -n No newline
No newline$ echo "No newline\c"
No newline$
```

The BSD variety of echo accepted the *option* -n, which suppressed the newline. AT&T's version used an *escape sequence*, \c, to do the same thing. Or was it the other way round? I have a hard time remembering which was which because, although I was using an AT&T system (hardware *and* operating system), its echo command accepted both AT&T and BSD syntax.

That, of course, is history. In this book, we're dealing with bash, so why does it matter? bash has the -e option to activate escape sequences such as \c but by default uses -n to prevent a newline from being printed. (The escape sequences recognized by echo -e are the same as those described in the next section, with the addition of \c.)

The trouble is that bash has an xpg_echo option (XPG stands for X/Open Portability Guide, a specification for Unix systems) that makes echo behave like that other version. This can be turned on or off while in the shell (using shopt -s xpg_echo either at the command line or in a script), or it can be turned on when the shell is compiled. In other words, even in bash, you cannot be absolutely sure which behavior you are going to get.

If you limit the use of echo to situations where there cannot be a conflict, that is, where you are sure the arguments do not begin with -n and do not contain escape sequences, you will be fairly safe. For everything else (or if you're not sure), use printf.

printf: Formatting and Printing Data

Derived from the C programming language function of the same name, the shell command printf is similar in purpose but differs in some of the details. Like the C function, it uses a format string to indicate how to present the rest of its arguments:

```
printf FORMAT ARG …
```

The FORMAT string can contain ordinary characters, escape sequences, and format specifiers. Ordinary characters are printed unchanged to the standard output. Escape sequences are converted to the characters they represent. Format specifiers are replaced with arguments from the command line.

Escape Sequences

Escape sequences are single letters preceded by a backslash:

- \a: : Alert (bell)
- \b: Backspace
- \e: Escape character
- \f: Form feed
- \n: Newline
- \r: Carriage return
- \t: Horizontal tab
- \v: Vertical tab
- \\: Backslash
- \nnn: A character specified by one to three octal digits
- \xHH: A character specified by one or two hexadecimal digits

The backslashes must be protected from the shell by quotes or another backslash:

```
$  printf "Q\t\141\n\x42\n"
Q       a
B
```

Format Specifiers

The format specifiers are letters preceded by a percent sign. Optional modifiers may be placed between the two characters. The specifiers are replaced by the corresponding argument. When there are more arguments than specifiers, the format string is reused until all the arguments have been consumed. The most commonly used specifiers are %s, %d, %f, and %x.

The %s specifier prints the literal characters in the argument:

```
$ printf "%s\n" Print arguments on "separate lines"
Print
arguments
on
separate lines
```

%b is like %s except that escape sequences in the arguments are translated:

```
$ printf "%b\n" "Hello\nworld" "12\tword"
Hello
world
12      word
```

Integers are printed with %d. The integer may be specified as a decimal, octal (using a leading 0), or hexadecimal (preceding the hex number with 0x) number. If the number is not a valid integer, printf prints an error message:

```
$ printf "%d\n" 23 45 56.78 0xff 011
23
45
bash: printf: 56.78: invalid number
0
255
9
```

For decimal fractions or floating-point numbers, use %f. By default they will be printed with six decimal places:

```
$ printf "%f\n" 12.34 23 56.789 1.2345678
12.340000
23.000000
56.789000
1.234568
```

Floating-point numbers can be presented in exponential (also known as *scientific*) notation using %e:

```
$ printf "%e\n" 12.34 23 56.789 123.45678
1.234000e+01
2.300000e+01
5.678900e+01
1.234568e+02
```

Integers can be printed in hexadecimal using %x for lowercase letters or %X for uppercase letters. For example, when specifying colors for a web page, they are specified in hex notation. I know from the rgb.txt file included with the X Window system that the red-green-blue values for royal blue are 65, 105, and 225. To convert them to a style rule for a web page, use this:

```
$ printf "color: #%02x%02x%02;x;\n" 65 105 225
color: #4169e1;
```

Width Specification

You can modify the formats by following the percent sign with a width specification. The argument will be printed flush right in a field of that width or will be flush left if the number is negative. Here we have the first field with a width of eight characters; the words will be printed flush right. Then there is a field 15 characters wide, which will be printed flush left:

```
$ printf "%8s %-15s:\n" first second third fourth fifth sixth
   first second      :
   third fourth      :
   fifth sixth       :
```

If the width specification is preceded by a 0, the numbers are padded with leading zeroes to fill the width:

```
$ printf "%04d\n" 12 23 56 123 255
0012
0023
0056
0123
0255
```

A width specifier with a decimal fraction specifies the precision of a floating-point number or the maximum width of a string:

```
$  printf "%12.4s %9.2f\n" John 2 Jackson 4.579 Walter 2.9
        John      2.00
        Jack      4.58
        Walt      2.90
```

The script shown in Listing 2-2 uses printf to output a simple sales report.

Listing 2-2. Report

```
#!/bin/bash
#: Description : print formatted sales report

## Build a long string of equals signs
divider=====================================
divider=$divider$divider

## Format strings for printf
header="\n %-10s %11s %8s %10s\n"
format=" %-10s %11.2f %8d %10.2f\n"

## Width of divider
totalwidth=44

## Print categories
printf "$header" ITEM  "PER UNIT" NUM TOTAL

## Print divider to match width of report
printf "%$totalwidth.${totalwidth}s\n" "$divider"

## Print lines of report
printf "$format" \
    Chair 79.95 4 319.8 \
    Table  209.99 1 209.99 \
    Armchair 315.49 2 630.98
```

The resulting report looks like this:

```
ITEM          PER UNIT     NUM      TOTAL
=========================================
Chair            79.95       4     319.80
Table           209.99       1     209.99
Armchair        315.49       2     630.98
```

Note the use of braces around the second `totalwidth` variable name: `${totalwidth}`. In the first instance, the name is followed by a period, which cannot be part of a variable name. In the second, it is followed by the letter s, which could be, so the `totalwidth` name must be separated from it by using braces.

Printing to a Variable

With version 3.1, `bash` added a `-v` option to store the output in a variable instead of printing it to the standard output:

```
$ printf -v num4 "%04d" 4
$ printf "%s\n" "$num4"
0004
```

Line Continuation

At the end of the `report` script, the last four lines are read as a single line, using *line continuation*. A backslash at the end of a line tells the shell to ignore the newline character, effectively joining the next line to the current one.

Standard Input/Output Streams and Redirection

In Unix (of which Linux is a variety), everything is a stream of bytes. The streams are accessible as files, but there are three streams that are rarely accessed by a filename. These are the input/output (I/O) streams attached to every command: standard input, standard output, and standard error. By default, these streams are connected to your terminal.

When a command reads a character or a line, it reads from the standard input stream, which is the keyboard. When it prints information, it is sent to the standard output, your monitor. The third stream, standard error, is also connected to your monitor; as the name implies, it is used for error messages. These streams are referred to by numbers, called *file descriptors* (FDs). These are 0, 1, and 2, respectively. The stream names are also often contracted to *stdin*, *stdout*, and *stderr*.

I/O streams can be redirected to (or from) a file or into a *pipeline*.

Redirection: >, >>, and <

In Chapter 1, you redirected standard output to a file using the > redirection operator.

When redirecting using >, the file is created if it doesn't exist. If it does exist, the file is truncated to zero length before anything is sent to it. You can create an empty file by redirecting an empty string (that is, nothing) to the file:

```
printf "" > FILENAME
```

or by simply using this:

```
> FILENAME
```

Redirection is performed before any command on the line is executed. If you redirect to the same file you are reading from, that file will be truncated, and the command will have nothing to read.

The >> operator doesn't truncate the destination file; it appends to it. You could add a line to the hw command from the first chapter by doing the following:

```
echo exit 0 >> bin/hw
```

Redirecting standard output does not redirect standard error. Error messages will still be displayed on your monitor. To send the error messages to a file, in other words, to redirect FD2, the redirection operator is preceded by the FD.

Both standard output and standard error can be redirected on the same line. The next command sends standard output to FILE and standard error to ERRORFILE:

```
$ printf '%s\n%v\n' OK? Oops! > FILE 2> ERRORFILE
$ cat ERRORFILE
bash4: printf: `v': invalid format character
```

In this case, the error message is going to a special file, /dev/null. Sometimes called the *bit bucket*, anything written to it is discarded.

```
printf '%s\n%v\n' OK? Oops! 2>/dev/null
```

Instead of sending output to a file, it can be redirected to another I/O stream by using >&N where N is the number of the file descriptor. This command sends both standard output and standard error to FILE:

```
printf '%s\n%v\n' OK? Oops! > FILE 2>&1
```

Here, the order is important. The standard output is sent to FILE, and then standard error is redirected to where standard output is going. If the order is reversed, the effect is different. The redirection sends standard error to wherever standard output is currently going and then changes where standard output goes. Standard error still goes to where standard output was originally directed:

```
printf '%s\n%v\n' OK? Oops! 2>&1 > FILE
```

bash has also a nonstandard syntax for redirecting both standard output and standard error to the same place:

```
&> FILE
```

To append both standard output and standard error to FILE, use this:

```
&>> FILE
```

A command that reads from standard input can have its input redirected from a file:

```
tr ,H wY < bin/hw
```

You can use the exec command to redirect the I/O streams for the rest of the script or until it's changed again.

All standard output will now go to the file tempfile, input will be read from datafile, and error messages will go to errorfile without having to specify it for every command.

Reading Input

The read command is a built-in shell that reads from the standard input. By default, it reads until a newline is received. The input is stored in one or more variables given as arguments:

```
read var
```

If more than one variable is given, the first word (the input up to the first space or tab) is assigned to the first variable, the second word is assigned to the second variable, and so on, with any leftover words assigned to the last one:

```
$ read a b c d
January February March April May June July August
$ echo $a
January
$ echo $b
February
$ echo $c
March
$ echo $d
April May June July August
```

The bash version of read has several options. Only the -r option is recognized by the POSIX standard. It tells the shell to interpret escape sequences literally.

By default, read strips backslashes from the input, and the following character is taken literally. The major effect of this default behavior is to allow the continuation of lines. With the -r option, a backslash followed by a newline is read as a literal backslash and the end of input.

I'll discuss the other options in Chapter 15.

Like any other command that reads standard input, read can get its input from a file through redirection. For example, to read the first line from FILENAME, use this:

```
read var < FILENAME
```

Pipelines

Pipelines connect the standard output of one command directly to the standard input of another. The pipe symbol (|) is used between the commands:

```
$ printf "%s\n" "$RANDOM" "$RANDOM" "$RANDOM" "$RANDOM" | tee FILENAME
618
11267
```

```
5890
8930
```

The tee command reads from the standard input and passes it to one or more files as well as to the standard output. $RANDOM is a bash variable that returns a different integer between 0 and 32,767 each time it is referenced.

```
$ cat FILENAME
618
11267
5890
8930
```

Command Substitution

The output of a command can be stored in a variable using *command substitution*. There are two forms for doing this. The first, which originated in the Bourne shell, uses backticks:

```
date=`date`
```

The newer (and recommended) syntax is as follows:

```
date=$( date )
```

Command substitution should generally be reserved for external commands. When used with a built-in command, it is very slow. That is why the -v option was added to printf.

Summary

The following are the commands and concepts you learned in this chapter.

Commands

- cat: Prints the contents of one or more files to the standard output
- tee: Copies the standard input to the standard output and one or more files
- read: A built-in shell command that reads a line from the standard input
- date: Prints the current date and time

Concepts

- *Standard I/O streams*: These are streams of bytes from which commands read and to which output is sent.
- *Arguments*: These are words that follow a command; arguments may include options as well as other information such as filenames.

- *Parameters*: These are entities that store values; the three types are positional parameters, special parameters, and variables.

- *Pipelines*: A pipeline is a sequence of one or more commands separated by |; the standard output of the command preceding the pipe symbol is fed to the standard input of the command following it.

- *Line continuation*: This is a backslash at the end of a line that removes the newline and combines that line with the next.

- *Command substitution*: This means storing the output of a command in a variable or on the command line.

Exercises

1. What is wrong with this command?

   ```
   tr A Z < $HOME/temp > $HOME/temp
   ```

2. Write a script, using $RANDOM, to write the following output both to a file and to a variable. The following numbers are only to show the format; your script should produce different numbers:

   ```
    1988.2365
   13798.14178
   10081.134
    3816.15098
   ```

■ ■ ■

## CHAPTER 3

Looping and Branching

At the heart of any programming language are iteration and conditional execution. *Iteration* is the repetition of a section of code until a condition changes. *Conditional execution* is making a choice between two or more actions (one of which may be to do nothing) based on a condition.

In the shell, there are three types of loop (while, until, and for) and three types of conditional execution (if, case, and the conditional operators && and ||, which mean AND and OR, respectively). With the exception of for and case, the exit status of a command controls the behavior.

Exit Status

You can test the success of a command directly using the shell keywords while, until, and if or with the control operators && and ||. The exit code is stored in the special parameter $?.

If the command executed successfully (or true), the value of $? is zero. If the command failed for some reason, $? will contain a positive integer between 1 and 255 inclusive. A failed command usually returns 1. Zero and nonzero exit codes are also known as *true* and *false*, respectively.

A command may fail because of a syntax error:

```
$ printf "%v\n"
bash: printf: `v': invalid format character
$ echo $?
1
```

Alternatively, failure may be the result of the command not being able to accomplish its task:

```
$ mkdir /qwerty
bash: mkdir: cannot create directory `/qwerty': Permission denied
$ echo $?
1
```

Testing an Expression

Expressions are deemed to be true or false by the test command or one of two nonstandard shell reserved words, [[and ((. The test command compares strings, integers, and various file attributes; ((tests arithmetic expressions, and [[...]] does the same as test with the additional feature of comparing regular expressions.

test, aka [...]

The test command evaluates many kinds of expressions, from file properties to integers to strings. It is a built-in command, and therefore its arguments are expanded just as for any other command. (See Chapter 5 for more information.) The alternative version ([) requires a closing bracket at the end.

File Tests

Several operators test the state of a file. A file's existence can be tested with -e (or the nonstandard -a). The type of file can be checked with -f for a regular file, -d for a directory, and -h or -L for a symbolic link. Other operators test for special types of files and for which permission bits are set.

Here are some examples:

```
test -f /etc/fstab     ## true if a regular file
test -h /etc/rc.local  ## true if a symbolic link
[ -x $HOME/bin/hw ]    ## true if you can execute the file
```

Integer Tests

Comparisons between integers use the -eq, -ne, -gt, -lt, -ge, and -le operators.

The equality of integers is tested with -eq:

```
$ test 1 -eq 1
$ echo $?
0
$ [ 2 -eq 1 ]
$ echo $?
1
```

Inequality is tested with -ne:

```
$ [ 2 -ne 1 ]
$ echo $?
0
```

The remaining operators test greater than, less than, greater than or equal to, and less than or equal to.

String Tests

Strings are concatenations of zero or more characters and can include any character except NUL (ASCII 0). They can be tested for equality or inequality, for nonempty string or null string, and in bash for alphabetical ordering. The = operator tests for equality, in other words, whether they are identical; != tests for inequality. bash also accepts == for equality, but there is no reason to use this nonstandard operator.

Here are some examples:

```
test "$a" = "$b"
[ "$q" != "$b" ]
```

The -z and -n operators return successfully if their arguments are empty or nonempty:

```
$ [ -z "" ]
$ echo $?
0
$ test -n ""
$ echo $?
1
```

The greater-than and less-than symbols are used in bash to compare the lexical positions of strings and must be escaped to prevent them from being interpreted as redirection operators:

```
$ str1=abc
$ str2=def
$ test "$str1" \< "$str2"
$ echo $?
0
$ test "$str1" \> "$str2"
$ echo $?
1
```

The previous tests can be combined in a single call to test with the -a (logical AND) and -o (logical OR) operators:

```
test -f /path/to/file -a $test -eq 1
test -x bin/file -o $test -gt 1
```

test is usually used in combination with if or the conditional operators && and ||.

[[...]]: Evaluate an Expression

Like test, [[...]] evaluates an expression. Unlike test, it is not a built-in command. It is part of the shell grammar and not subject to the same parsing as a built-in command. Parameters are expanded, but word splitting and file name expansion are not performed on words between [[and]].

It supports all the same operators as test, with some enhancements and additions. It is, however, nonstandard, so it is better not to use it when test could perform the same function.

Enhancements over Test

When the argument to the right of = or != is unquoted, it is treated as a pattern and duplicates the functionality of the case command.

The feature of [[...]] that is not duplicated elsewhere in the shell is the ability to match an extended regular expression using the =~ operator:

```
$ string=whatever
$ [[ $string =~ h[aeiou] ]]
$ echo $?
0
```

```
$ [[ $string =~ h[sdfghjkl] ]]
$ echo $?
1
```

Regular expressions are explained in Chapter 8.

((...)): Evaluate an Arithmetic Expression

A nonstandard feature, ((arithmetic expression)) returns false if the arithmetic expression evaluates to zero and returns true otherwise. The portable equivalent uses test and the POSIX syntax for shell arithmetic:

```
test $(( $a - 2 )) -ne 0
```

Lists

A *list* is a sequence of one or more commands separated by semicolons, ampersands, control operators, or newlines. A list may be used as the condition in a while or until loop or as the body of any loop. The exit code of a list is the exit code of the last command in the list.

Conditional execution

Conditional constructs enable a script to decide whether to execute a block of code or to select which of two or more blocks to execute.

if

The basic if command evaluates a list of one or more commands and executes a list if the execution of <condition list> is successful:

```
if <condition list>
then
    <list>
fi
```

Usually, the <condition list> is a single command, very often test or its synonym, [. In Listing 3-1, the -z operand to test checks whether a name was entered.

Listing 3-1. Read and Check Input

```
read name
if [ -z "$name" ]
then
    echo "No name entered" >&2
    exit 1  ## Set a failed return code
fi
```

Using the else keyword, a different set of commands can be executed if the <condition list> fails, as shown in Listing 3-2.

Listing 3-2. Prompt for a Number and Check That It Is No Greater Than Ten

```
printf "Enter a number no greater than 10: "
read number
if [ "$number" -gt 10 ]
then
    printf "%d is too big\n" "$number" >&2
    exit 1
else
    printf "You entered %d\n" "$number"
fi
```

More than one condition can be given, using the elif keyword, so that if the first test fails, the second is tried, as shown in Listing 3-3.

Listing 3-3. Prompt for a Number and Check That It Is Within a Given Range

```
printf "Enter a number between 10 and 20 inclusive: "
read number
if [ "$number" -lt 10 ]
then
    printf "%d is too low\n" "$number" >&2
    exit 1
elif [ "$number" -gt 20 ]
then
    printf "%d is too high\n" "$number" >&2
    exit 1
else
    printf "You entered %d\n" "$number"
fi
```

■ **Note** In real use, a number entered in the previous examples would be checked for invalid characters before its value is compared. Code to do that is given in the "case" section.

Often more than one test is given in the <condition list> using && and ||.

Conditional Operators, && and ||

Lists containing the AND and OR conditional operators are evaluated from left to right. A command following the AND operator (&&) is executed if the previous command is successful. The part following the OR operator (||) is executed if the previous command fails.

For example, to check for a directory and cd into it if it exists, use this:

```
test -d "$directory" && cd "$directory"
```

To change directory and exit with an error if cd fails, use this:

```
cd "$HOME/bin" || exit 1
```

The next command tries to create a directory and cd to it. If either mkdir or cd fails, it exits with an error:

```
mkdir "$HOME/bin" && cd "$HOME/bin" || exit 1
```

Conditional operators are often used with if. In this example, the echo command is executed if both tests are successful:

```
if [ -d "$dir" ] && cd "$dir"
then
    echo "$PWD"
fi
```

case

A case statement compares a word (usually a variable) against one or more patterns and executes the commands associated with that pattern. The patterns are pathname expansion patterns using wildcards (* and ?) and character lists and ranges ([…]). The syntax is as follows:

```
case WORD in
  PATTERN) COMMANDS ;;
  PATTERN) COMMANDS ;; ## optional
esac
```

A common use of case is to determine whether one string is contained in another. It is much faster than using grep, which creates a new process. This short script would normally be implemented as a shell function (see Chapter 6) so that it will be executed without creating a new process, as shown in Listing 3-4.

Listing 3-4. Does One String Contain Another?

```
case $1 in
    *"$2"*) true ;;
    *) false ;;
esac
```

The commands, true and false, do nothing but succeed or fail, respectively.

Another common task is to check whether a string is a valid number. Again, Listing 3-5 would usually be implemented as a function.

Listing 3-5. Is This a Valid Integer?

```
case $1 in
    *[!0-9]*) false;;
    *) true ;;
esac
```

Many scripts require one or more arguments on the command line. To check whether there are the correct number, case is often used:

```
case $# in
    3) ;; ## We need 3 args, so do nothing
    *) printf "%s\n" "Please provide three names" >&2
       exit 1
       ;;
esac
```

Looping

When a command or series of commands needs to be repeated, it is put inside a loop. The shell provides three types of loop: while, until, and for. The first two execute until a condition is either true or false; the third loops through a list of words.

while

The condition for a while loop is a list of one or more commands, and the commands to be executed while the condition remains true are placed between the keywords do and done:

```
while <list>
do
  <list>
done
```

By incrementing a variable each time the loop is executed, the commands can be run a specific number of times:

```
n=1
while [ $n -le 10 ]
do
  echo "$n"
  n=$(( $n + 1 ))
done
```

The true command can be used to create an infinite loop:

```
while true ## : can be used in place of true
do
  read x
done
```

A while loop can be used to read line by line from a file:

```
while IFS= read -r line
do
  : do something with "$line"
done < FILENAMEy?
```

until

Rarely used, until loops as long as the condition fails. It is the opposite of while:

```
n=1
until [ $n -gt 10 ]
do
  echo "$n"
  n=$(( $n + 1 ))
done
```

for

At the top of a for loop, a variable is given a value from a list of words. On each iteration, the next word in the list is assigned:

```
for var in Canada USA Mexico
do
  printf "%s\n" "$var"
done
```

bash also has a nonstandard form that is similar to that found in the C programming language. The first expression is evaluated when first encountered. The second is a test. The third is evaluated after each iteration:

```
for (( n=1; n<=10; ++n ))
do
  echo "$n"
done
```

Since this offers no advantage over standard looping methods, it is not used in this book.

break

A loop can be exited at any point with the break command:

```
while :
do
  read x
  [ -z "$x" ] && break
done
```

With a numeric argument, break can exit multiple nested loops:

```
for n in a b c d e
do
  while true
  do
    if [ $RANDOM -gt 20000 ]
    then
      printf .
      break 2 ## break out of both while and for loops
    elif [ $RANDOM -lt 10000 ]
    then
      printf '"'
      break ## break out of the while loop
    fi
  done
done
echo
```

continue

Inside a loop, the continue command immediately starts a new iteration of the loop, bypassing any remaining commands:

```
for n in {1..9} ## See Brace expansion in Chapter 4
do
  x=$RANDOM
  [ $x -le 20000 ] && continue
  echo "n=$n x=$x"
done
```

Summary

Looping and branching are major building blocks of a computer program. In this chapter, you learned the commands and operators used for these tasks.

Commands

- test: Evaluates an expression and returns success or failure
- if: Executes a set of command if a list of commands is successful and optionally executes a different set if it is not
- case: Matches a word with one or more patterns and executes the commands associated with the first matching pattern
- while: Repeatedly executes a set of commands while a list of commands executes successfully

- until: Repeatedly executes a set of commands until a list of commands executes successfully

- for: Repeatedly executes a set of commands for each word in a list

- break: Exits from a loop

- continue: Starts the next iteration of a loop immediately

Concepts

- *Exit status*: The success or failure of a command, stored as 0 or a positive integer in the special parameter $?

- *List*: A sequence of one or more commands separated by ;, &, &&, ||, or a newline

Exercises

1. Write a script that asks the user to enter a number between 20 and 30. If the user enters an invalid number or a non-number, ask again. Repeat until a satisfactory number is entered.

2. Write a script that prompts the user to enter the name of a file. Repeat until the user enters a file that exists.

CHAPTER 4

■ ■ ■

Command-Line Parsing and Expansion

One of the strengths of the shell as a programming language is its parsing of command-line arguments and the various expansions it performs on words in the line. When a command is called with arguments, the shell does several things before it invokes the command.

To help visualize what happens, the short script shown in Listing 4-1, called sa, will display what the shell has passed to it after processing all the arguments. Each of its arguments is printed on a separate line, preceded by the value of $pre and followed by the value of $post.

Listing 4-1. sa; Displaying Command-Line Arguments

```
pre=:
post=:
printf "$pre%s$post\n" "$@"
```

The special parameter $@ expands to a list of all the command-line arguments, but the results differ depending on whether it is quoted. When quoted, it expands to the positional parameters "$1", "$2", "$3", "$4", and so on, and the arguments containing whitespace will be preserved. If $@ is unquoted, splitting will occur wherever there is whitespace.

When a line is executed, whether at the command prompt or in a script, the shell splits the line into words wherever there is unquoted whitespace. Then bash examines the resulting words, performing up to eight types of expansion on them as appropriate. The results of the expansions are passed to the command as its arguments. This chapter examines the entire process, from the initial parsing into words based on unquoted whitespace to each of the expansions in the order in which they are performed:

1. Brace expansion

2. Tilde expansion

3. Parameter and variable expansion

4. Arithmetic expansion

5. Command substitution

6. Word splitting

7. Pathname expansion

8. Process substitution

The chapter ends with a shell program that demonstrates how to parse options (arguments beginning with a hyphen) on the command line, using the getopts built-in command.

Quoting

The shell's initial parsing of the command line uses unquoted whitespace, that is, spaces, tabs, and newlines, to separate the words. Spaces between single or double quotes or spaces preceded by the escape character (\) are considered part of the surrounding word if any. The delimiting quotation marks are stripped from the arguments.

The following code has five arguments. The first is the word this preceded by a space (the backslash removes its special meaning). The second argument is is a; the entire argument is enclosed in double quotes, again removing the special meaning from the space. The phrase, demonstration of, is enclosed in single quotes. Next is a single, escaped space. Finally, the string quotes and escapes is held together by the escaped spaces.

```
$ sa \ this "is a" 'demonstration of' \  quotes\ and\ escapes
: this:
:is a:
:demonstration of:
: :
:quotes and escapes:
```

Quotes can be embedded in a word. Inside double quotes, a single quote is not special, but a double quote must be escaped. Inside single quotes, a double quote is not special.

```
$ sa "a double-quoted single quote, '" "a double-quoted double quote, \""
:a double-quoted single quote, ':
:a double-quoted double quote, ":
$ sa 'a single-quoted double quotation mark, "'
:a single-quoted double quotation mark, ":
```

All characters inside a single-quoted word are taken literally. A single-quoted word cannot contain a single quote even if it is escaped; the quotation mark will be regarded as closing the preceding one, and another single quote opens a new quoted section. Consecutive quoted words without any intervening whitespace are considered as a single argument:

```
$ sa "First argument "'still the first argument'
:First argument still the first argument:
```

In bash, single quotes can be included in words of the form $'string' if they are escaped. In addition, the escape sequences listed in Chapter 2's description of printf are replaced by the characters they represent:

```
$ echo $'\'line1\'\n\'line2\''
'line1'
'line2'
```

Quoted arguments can contain literal newlines:

```
$ sa "Argument containing
> a newline"
:Argument containing
a newline:
```

Brace Expansion

The first expansion performed, brace expansion, is nonstandard (that is, it is not included in the POSIX specification). It operates on unquoted braces containing either a comma-separated list or a sequence. Each element becomes a separate argument.

```
$ sa {one,two,three}
:one:
:two:
:three:
$ sa {1..3} ## added in bash3.0
:1:
:2:
:3:
$ sa {a..c}
:a:
:b:
:c:
```

A string before or after the brace expression will be included in each expanded argument:

```
$ sa pre{d,l}ate
:predate:
:prelate:
```

Braces may be nested:

```
$ sa {{1..3},{a..c}}
:1:
:2:
:3:
:a:
:b:
:c:
```

Multiple braces within the same word are expanded recursively. The first brace expression is expanded, and then each of the resulting words is processed for the next brace expression. With the word {1..3}{a..c}, the first term is expanded, giving the following:

```
1{a..c} 2{a..c} 3{a..c}
```

Each of these words is then expanded for this final result:

```
$ sa {1..3}{a..c}
:1a:
:1b:
:1c:
:2a:
:2b:
:2c:
:3a:
:3b:
:3c:
```

In version 4 of bash, further capabilities have been added to brace expansion. Numerical sequences can be padded with zeros, and the increment in a sequence can be specified:

```
$ sa {01..13..3}
:01:
:04:
:07:
:10:
:13:
```

Increments can also be used with alphabetic sequences:

```
$ sa {a..h..3}
:a:
:d:
:g:
```

Tilde Expansion

An unquoted tilde expands to the user's home directory:

```
$ sa ~
:/home/chris:
```

Followed by a login name, it expands to that user's home directory:

```
$ sa ~root ~chris
:/root:
:/home/chris:
```

When quoted, either on the command line or in a variable assignment, the tilde is not expanded:

```
$ sa "~" "~root"
:~:
:~root:
$ dir=~chris
$ dir2="~chris"
$ sa "$dir" "$dir2"
:/home/chris:
:~chris:
```

If the name following the tilde is not a valid login name, no expansion is performed:

```
$ sa ~qwerty
:~qwerty:
```

Parameter and Variable Expansion

Parameter expansion replaces a variable with its contents; it is introduced by a dollar sign ($). It is followed by the symbol or name to be expanded:

```
$ var=whatever
$ sa "$var"
:whatever:
```

The parameter may be enclosed in braces:

```
$ var=qwerty
$ sa "${var}"
:qwerty:
```

In most cases, the braces are optional. They are required when referring to a positional parameter greater than nine or when a variable name is followed immediately by a character that could be part of a name:

```
$ first=Jane
$ last=Johnson
$ sa "$first_$last" "${first}_$last"
:Johnson:
:Jane_Johnson:
```

Because first_ is a valid variable name, the shell tries to expand it rather than first; adding the braces removes the ambiguity.

Braces are also used in expansions that do more than simply return the value of a parameter. These often-cryptic expansions (${var##*/} and ${var//x/y}, for example) add a great deal of power to the shell and are examined in detail in the next chapter.

Parameter expansions that are not enclosed in double quotes are subject to *word splitting* and *pathname expansion*.

Arithmetic Expansion

When the shell encounters $((expression)), it evaluates expression and places the result on the command line; expression is an arithmetic expression. Besides the four basic arithmetic operations of addition, subtraction, multiplication, and division, its most used operator is % (modulo, the remainder after division).

```
$ sa "$(( 1 + 12 ))" "$(( 12 * 13 ))" "$(( 16 / 4 ))" "$(( 6 - 9 ))"
:13:
:156:
:4:
:-3:
```

The arithmetic operators (see Tables 4-1 and 4-2) take the same precedence that you learned in school (basically, that multiplication and division are performed before addition and subtraction), and they can be grouped with parentheses to change the order of evaluation:

```
$ sa "$(( 3 + 4 * 5 ))" "$(( (3 + 4) * 5 ))"
:23:
:35:
```

The modulo operator, %, returns the remainder after division:

```
$ sa "$(( 13 % 5 ))"
:3:
```

Converting seconds (which is how Unix systems store times) to days, hours, minutes, and seconds involves division and the modulo operator, as shown in Listing 4-2.

Listing 4-2. secs2dhms, Convert Seconds (in Argument $1) to Days, Hours, Minutes, and Seconds

```
secs_in_day=86400
secs_in_hour=3600
mins_in_hour=60
secs_in_min=60

days=$(( $1 / $secs_in_day ))
secs=$(( $1 % $secs_in_day ))
printf "%d:%02d:%02d:%02d\n" "$days" "$(($secs / $secs_in_hour))" \
       "$((($secs / $mins_in_hour) %$mins_in_hour))" "$(($secs % $secs_in_min))"
```

If not enclosed in double quotes, the results of arithmetic expansion are subject to *word splitting*.

Table 4-1. Arithmetic Operators

Operator	Description
- +	Unary minus and plus
! ~	Logical and bitwise negation
* / %	Multiplication, division, remainder
+ -	Addition, subtraction
<< >>	Left and right bitwise shifts
<= >= < >	Comparison
== !=	Equality and inequality

Operator	Description
&	Bitwise AND
^	Bitwise exclusive OR
|	Bitwise OR
&&	Logical AND
||	Logical OR
= *= /= %= += -= <<= >>= &= ^= |=	Assignment

Table 4-2. bash Extensions

Operator	Description
**	Exponentiation
id++ id--	Variable post-increment and post-decrement
++id --id	Variable pre-increment and pre-decrement
expr ? expr1 : expr2	Conditional operator
expr1 , expr2	Comma

Command Substitution

Command substitution replaces a command with its output. The command must be placed either between backticks (` command `) or between parentheses preceded by a dollar sign ($(command)). For example, to count the lines in a file whose name includes today's date, this command uses the output of the date command:

```
$ wc -l $( date +%Y-%m-%d ).log
61 2009-03-31.log
```

The old format for command substitution uses backticks. This command is the same as the previous one:

```
$ wc -l `date +%Y-%m-%d`.log
2 2009-04-01.log
```

Well, it's not exactly the same, because I ran the first command shortly before midnight and the second shortly after. As a result, wc processed two different files.

If the command substitution is not quoted, *word splitting* and *pathanme expansion* are performed on the results.

Word Splitting

The results of parameter and arithmetic expansions, as well as command substitution, are subjected to word splitting if they were not quoted:

```
$ var="this is a multiword value"
$ sa $var "$var"
:this:
:is:
:a:
:multi-word:
:value:
:this is a multi-word value:
```

Word splitting is based on the value of the internal field separator variable, IFS. The default value of IFS contains the whitespace characters of space, tab, and newline (IFS=$' \t\n'). When IFS has its default value or is unset, any sequence of default IFS characters is read as a single delimiter.

```
$ var='    spaced
    out    '
$ sa $var
:spaced:
:out:
```

If IFS contains another character (or characters) as well as whitespace, then any sequence of whitespace characters plus that character will delimit a field, but every instance of a nonwhitespace character delimits a field:

```
S IFS=' :'
$ var="qwerty  : uiop :  :: er " ## :  :: delimits 2 empty fields
$ sa $var
:qwerty:
:uiop:
::
::
:er:
```

If IFS contains only nonwhitespace characters, then every occurrence of every character in IFS delimits a field, and whitespace is preserved:

```
$ IFS=:
$ var="qwerty  : uiop :  :: er "
$ sa $var
:qwerty  :
: uiop :
:  :
::
: er :
```

Pathname Expansion

Unquoted words on the command line containing the characters *, ?, and [are treated as *file globbing patterns* and are replaced by an alphabetical list of files that match the pattern. If no files match the pattern, the word is left unchanged.

The asterisk matches any string. h* matches all files in the current directory that begin with h, and *k matches all files that end with k. The shell replaces the wildcard pattern with the list of matching files in alphabetical order. If there are no matching files, the wildcard pattern is left unchanged.

```
$ cd "$HOME/bin"
$ sa h*
:hello:
:hw:
$ sa *k
:incheck:
:numcheck:
:rangecheck:
```

A question mark matches any single character; the following pattern matches all files whose second letter is a:

```
$ sa ?a*
:rangecheck:
:sa:
:valint:
:valnum:
```

Square brackets match any one of the enclosed characters, which may be a list, a range, or a class of characters: [aceg] matches any one of a, c, e, or g; [h-o] matches any character from h to o inclusive; and [[:lower:]] matches all lowercase letters.

You can disable file name expansion with the set -f command. bash has a number of options that affect file name expansion. I'll cover them in detail in Chapter 8.

Process Substitution

Process substitution creates a temporary filename for a command or list of commands. You can use it anywhere a file name is expected. The form <(command) makes the output of command available as a file name; >(command) is a file name that can be written to.

```
$ sa <(ls -l) >(pr -Tn)
:/dev/fd/63:
:/dev/fd/62:
```

■ **Note** The pr command converts text files for printing by inserting page headers. The headers can be turned off with the -T option, and the -n option numbers the lines.

When the file name on the command line is read, it produces the output of the command. Process substitution can be used in place of a pipeline, allowing variables defined within a loop to be visible to the rest of the script. In this snippet, totalsize is not available to the script outside the loop:

```
$ ls -l |
> while read perms links owner group size month day time file
> do
>   totalsize=$(( ${totalsize:=0} + ${size:-0} ))
> done
$   echo ${totalsize-unset} ## print "unset" if variable is not set
unset
```

By using process substitution instead, it becomes available:

```
$ while read perms links owner group size month day time file
> do
>   printf "%10d %s\n" "$size" "$file"
>   totalsize=$(( ${totalsize:=0} + ${size:-0} ))
> done < <(ls -l *)
$ echo ${totalsize-unset}
12879
```

Parsing Options

The options to a shell script, single characters preceded by a hyphen, can be parsed with the built-in command getopts. There may be arguments to some options, and options must precede nonoption arguments.

Multiple options may be concatenated with a single hyphen, but any that take an argument must be the final option in the string. Its argument follows, with or without intervening whitespace.

On the following command line, there are two options, -a and -f. The latter takes a file name argument. John is the first nonoption argument, and -x is not an option because it comes after a nonoption argument.

```
myscript -a -f filename John -x Jane
```

The syntax for getopts is as follows:

```
getopts OPTSTRING var
```

The OPTSTRING contains all the option's characters; those that take arguments are followed by a colon. For the script in Listing 4-3, the string is f:v. Each option is placed in the variable $var, and the option's argument, if any, is placed in $OPTARG.

Usually used as the condition to a while loop, getopts returns successfully until it has parsed all the options on the command line or until it encounters the word --. All remaining words on the command line are arguments passed to the main part of the script.

A frequently used option is -v to turn on verbose mode, which displays more than the default information about the running of the script. Other options—for example, -f—require a file name argument.

This sample script processes both the -v and -f options and, when in verbose mode, displays some information.

Listing 4-3. parseopts, Parse Command-Line Options

```
progname=${0##*/} ## Get the name of the script without its path

## Default values
verbose=0
filename=

## List of options the program will accept;
## those options that take arguments are followed by a colon
optstring=f:v

## The loop calls getopts until there are no more options on the command line
## Each option is stored in $opt, any option arguments are stored in OPTARG
while getopts $optstring opt
do
  case $opt in
    f) filename=$OPTARG ;; ## $OPTARG contains the argument to the option
    v) verbose=$(( $verbose + 1 )) ;;
    *) exit 1 ;;
  esac
done

## Remove options from the command line
## $OPTIND points to the next, unparsed argument
shift "$(( $OPTIND - 1 ))"

## Check whether a filename was entered
if [ -n "$filename" ]
then
   if [ $verbose -gt 0 ]
   then
      printf "Filename is %s\n" "$filename"
   fi
else
   if [ $verbose -gt 0 ]
   then
      printf "No filename entered\n" >&2
   fi
   exit 1
fi

## Check whether file exists
if [ -f "$filename" ]
then
  if [ $verbose -gt 0 ]
  then
    printf "Filename %s found\n" "$filename"
  fi
```

```
else
  if [ $verbose -gt 0 ]
  then
    printf "File, %s, does not exist\n" "$filename" >&2
  fi
  exit 2
fi

## If the verbose option is selected,
## print the number of arguments remaining on the command line
if [ $verbose -gt 0 ]
then
  printf "Number of arguments is %d\n" "$#"
fi
```

Running the script without any arguments does nothing except generate a failing return code:

```
$ parseopts
$ echo $?
1
```

With the verbose option, it prints an error message as well:

```
$ parseopts -v
No filename entered
$ echo $?
1
```

With an illegal option (that is, one that is not in $optstring), the shell prints an error message:

```
$ parseopts -x
/home/chris/bin/parseopts: illegal option - x
```

If a file name is entered and the file doesn't exist, it produces this:

```
$ parseopts -vf qwerty; echo $?
Filename is qwerty
File, qwerty, does not exist
2
```

To allow a nonoption argument to begin with a hyphen, the options can be explicitly ended with --:

```
$ parseopts -vf ~/.bashrc -- -x
Filename is /home/chris/.bashrc
Filename /home/chris/.bashrc found
Number of arguments is 1
```

Summary

The shell's preprocessing of the command line before passing it to a command saves the programmer a great deal of work.

Commands

- head: Extracts the first N lines from a file; N defaults to 10

- cut: Extracts columns from a file

Exercises

1. How many arguments are there on this command line?

    ```
    sa $# $(date "+%Y %m %d") John\ Doe
    ```

2. What potential problem exists with the following snippet?

    ```
    year=$( date +%Y )
    month=$( date +%m )
    day=$( date +%d )
    hour=$( date +%H )
    minute=$( date +%M )
    second=$( date +%S )
    ```

## CHAPTER 5

Parameters and Variables

Variables have been part of the Unix shell since its inception more than 30 years ago, but their features have grown over the years. The standard Unix shell now has parameter expansions that perform sophisticated manipulations on their contents. Bash adds even more expansion capabilities as well as indexed and associative arrays.

This chapter covers what you can do with variables and parameters, including their scope. In other words, after a variable has been defined, where can its value be accessed? This chapter gives a glimpse of the more than 80 variables used by the shell that are available to the programmer. It discusses how to name your variables and how to pick them apart with parameter expansion.

Positional parameters are the arguments passed to a script. They can be manipulated with the shift command and used individually by number or in a loop.

Arrays assign more than one value to a name. Bash has both numerically indexed arrays and, beginning with bash-4.0, associative arrays that are assigned and referenced by a string instead of a number.

The Scope of a Variable: Can You See It from Here?

By default, a variable's definition is known only to the shell in which it is defined (and to subshells of that shell). The script that called the current script will not know about it, and a script called by the current script will not know about the variable unless it is exported to the *environment*.

The environment is an array of strings of the form name=value. Whenever an external command is executed (creating a child process), whether it is a compiled, binary command or an interpreted script, this array is passed to it behind the scenes. In a shell script, these strings are available as variables.

Variables assigned in a script may be exported to the environment using the shell builtin command export:

```
var=whatever
export var
```

There is no need to export a variable unless you want to make it available to scripts (or other programs) called from the current script (and their children and *their* children's children and...). Exporting a variable doesn't make it visible anywhere except child processes.

Listing 5-1 tells you whether the variable $x is in the environment and what it contains, if anything.

Listing 5-1. showvar, Print Value of Variable x

```
if [ "${x+X}" = X ] ## If $x is set
then
  if [ -n "$x" ] ## if $x is not empty
```

```
then
  printf "  \$x = %s\n" "$x"
else
  printf "  \$x is set but empty\n"
fi
else
  printf " %s is not set\n" "\$x"
fi
```

Once a variable is exported, it remains in the environment until it is unset:

```
$ unset x
$ showvar
  $x is not set
$ x=3
$ showvar
  $x is not set
$ export x
$ showvar
  $x = 3
$ x= ## in bash, reassignment doesn't remove a variable from the environment
$ showvar
  $x is set but empty
```

Variables set in a subshell are not visible to the script that called it. Subshells include command substitution, as in $(command); all elements of a pipeline; and code enclosed in parentheses, as in (command).

Probably the most frequently asked question about shell programming is, "Where did my variables go? I know I set them, so why are they empty?" More often than not, this is caused by piping the output of one command into a loop that assigns variables:

```
printf "%s\n" ${RANDOM}{,,,,,} |
  while read num
  do
    [ $num -gt ${biggest:=0} ] && biggest=$num
  done
printf "The largest number is: %d\n" "$biggest"
```

When biggest is found to be empty, complaints of variables set in while loops not being available outside them are heard in all the shell forums. But the problem is not the loop; it is that the loop is part of a pipeline and therefore is being executed in a subshell.

Shell Variables

The shell either sets or uses more than 80 variables. Many of these are used by bash internally and are of little use to shell programmers. Others are used in debugging, and some are in common use in shell programs. About half are set by the shell itself, and the rest are set by the operating system, the user, the terminal, or a script.

Of those set by the shell, you have already looked at RANDOM, which returns a random integer between 0 and 32,767, and PWD, which contains the path to the current working directory. You saw OPTIND and OPTARG used in parsing command-line options (Chapter 4). Sometimes, BASH_VERSION (or

BASH_VERSINFO) is used to determine whether the running shell is capable of running a script. Some of the scripts in this book require at least bash-3.0 and might use one of those variables to determine whether the current shell is recent enough to run the script:

```
case $BASH_VERSION in
  [12].*) echo "You need at least bash3.0 to run this script" >&2; exit 2;;
esac
```

The prompt string variables, PS1 and PS2, are used in interactive shells at the command line; PS3 is used with the select builtin command, and PS4 is printed before each line in execution trace mode (more on that in Chapter 10).

SHELL VARIABLES

The following variables are set by the shell:

BASH	COMP_KEY	OLDPWD
BASHPID	COMP_LINE	OPTARG
BASH_ALIASES	COMP_POINT	OPTIND
BASH_ARGC	COMP_TYPE	OSTYPE
BASH_ARGV	COMP_WORDBREAKS	PIPESTATUS
BASH_CMDS	COMP_WORDS	PPID
BASH_COMMAND	DIRSTACK	PWD
BASH_EXECUTION_STRING	EUID	RANDOM
BASH_LINENO	FUNCNAME	REPLY
BASH_REMATCH	GROUPS	SECONDS
BASH_SOURCE	HISTCMD	SHELLOPTS
BASH_SUBSHELL	HOSTNAME	SHLVL
BASH_VERSINFO	HOSTTYPE	UID
BASH_VERSION	LINENO	
COMP_CWORD	MACHTYPE	

The following variables are used by the shell, which may set a default value for some of them (for example, IFS):

BASH_ENV	HISTIGNORE	LC_CTYPE	PROMPT_DIRTRIM
CDPATH	HISTSIZE	LC_MESSAGES	PS1
COLUMNS	HISTTIMEFORMAT	LC_NUMERIC	PS2
COMPREPLY	HOME	LINES	PS3
EMACS	HOSTFILE	MAIL	PS4
FCEDIT	IFS	MAILCHECK	SHELL
FIGNORE	IGNOREEOF	MAILPATH	TIMEFORMAT
GLOBIGNORE	INPUTRC	OPTERR	TMOUT
HISTCONTROL	LANG	PATH	TMPDIR
HISTFILE	LC_ALL	POSIXLY_CORRECT	auto_resume
HISTFILESIZE	LC_COLLATE	PROMPT_COMMAND	histchars

See the appendix for a description of all the shell variables.

The Naming of Variables

Variable names can contain only letters, numbers, and underscores, and they must start with a letter or an underscore. Apart from those restrictions, you are free to build your names as you see fit. It is, however, a good idea to use a consistent scheme for naming variables, and choosing meaningful names can go a long way toward making your code self-documenting.

Perhaps the most frequently cited (though less often implemented) convention is that environment variables should be in capital letters, while local variables should be in lowercase. Given that bash itself uses more than 80 uppercase variables internally, this is a dangerous practice, and conflicts are not uncommon. I have seen variables such as PATH, HOME, LINES, SECONDS, and UID misused with potentially disastrous consequences. None of bash's variables begin with an underscore, so in my first book, *Shell Scripting Recipes: A Problem-Solution Approach* (Apress, 2005), I used uppercase names preceded by an underscore for values set by shell functions.

Single-letter names should be used rarely. They are appropriate as the index in a loop, where its sole function is as a counter. The letter traditionally used for this purpose is i, but I prefer n. (When teaching programming in a classroom, the letter I on the blackboard was too easily confused with the number 1, so I started using n for "number," and I still use it 20 years later.)

The only other place I use single-letter variable names is when reading throwaway material from a file. If I need only one or two fields from a file, for example, I use this:

```
while IFS=: read login a b c name e
do
  printf "%-12s %s\n" "$login" "$name"
done < /etc/passwd
```

I recommend two naming schemes. The first is used by Heiner Steven on his Shelldorado web site at http://www.shelldorado.com/. He capitalizes the first letter of all variables and also the first letters of further words in the name: ConfigFile, LastDir, FastMath. In some cases, his usage is closer to mine.

I use all lowercase letters: configfile, lastdir, fastmath. When the run-together words are ambiguous or hard to read, I separate them with an underscore: line_width, bg_underline, day_of_week.

Whatever system you choose, the important thing is that the names give a real indication of what the variable contains. But don't get carried away and use something like this:

```
long_variable_name_which_may_tell_you_something_about_its_purpose=1
```

Parameter Expansion

Much of the power of the modern Unix shell comes from its parameter expansions. In the Bourne shell, these mostly involved testing whether a parameter is set or empty and replacing with a default or alternate value. KornShell additions, which were incorporated into the POSIX standard, added string manipulation. KornShell 93 added more expansions that have not been incorporated into the standard but that bash has adopted. Bash-4.0 has added two new expansions of its own.

Bourne Shell

The Bourne shell and its successors have expansions to replace an empty or unset variable with a default, to assign a default value to a variable if it is empty or unset, and to halt execution and print an error message if a variable is empty or unset.

${var:-default} and ${var-default}: Use Default Values

The most commonly used expansion, ${var:-default}, checks to see whether a variable is unset or empty and expands to a default string if it is:

```
$ var=
$ sa "${var:-default}"  ## The sa script was introduced in Chapter 4
:default:
```

If the colon is omitted, the expansion checks only whether the variable is unset:

```
$ var=
$ sa "${var-default}" ## var is set, so expands to nothing
::
$ unset var
$ sa "${var-default}" ## var is unset, so expands to "default"
:default:
```

This snippet assigns a default value to $filename if it is not supplied by an option or inherited in the environment:

```
defaultfile=$HOME/.bashrc
## parse options here
filename=${filename:-"$defaultfile"}
```

${var:+alternate}, ${var+alternate}: Use Alternate Values

The complement to the previous expansion substitutes an alternate value if the parameter is not empty or, without a colon, if it is set. The first expansion will use alternate only if $var is set and is not empty:

```
$ var=
$ sa "${var:+alternate}" ## $var is set but empty
::
$ var=value
$ sa "${var:+alternate}" ## $var is not empty
:alernate:
```

Without the colon, alternate is used if the variable is set, even if it is empty:

```
$ var=
$ sa "${var+alternate}" ## var is set
:altername:
$ unset var
$ sa "${var+alternate}" ## $var is not set
::
$ var=value
$ sa "${var:+alternate}" ## $var is set and not empty
:alternate:
```

This expansion is often used when adding strings to a variable. If the variable is empty, you don't want to add a separator:

```
$ var=
$ for n in a b c d e f g
> do
>     var="$var $n"
> done
$ sa "$var"
: a b c d e f g:
```

To prevent the leading space, you can use parameter expansion:

```
$ var=
$ for n in a b c d e f g
> do
>     var="${var:+"$var "}$n"
> done
$ sa "$var"
:a b c d e f g:
```

That is a shorthand method of doing the following for each value of n:

```
if [ -n "$var" ]
then
  var="$var $n"
else
  var=$n
fi
```

or:

```
[ -n "$var" ] && var="$var $n" || var=$n
```

${var:=default}, ${var=default}: Assign Default Values

The ${var:=default} expansion behaves in the same way as ${var:-default} except that it also assigns the default value to the variable:

```
$ unset n
$ while :
> do
>   echo :$n:
>   [ ${n:=0} -gt 3 ] && break ## set $n to 0 if unset or empty
>   n=$(( $n + 1 ))
> done
::
:1:
:2:
:3:
:4:
```

${var:?message}, ${var?message}: Display Error Message If Empty or Unset

If var is empty or not set, message will be printed to the standard error, and the script will exit with a status of 1. If message is empty, parameter null or not set will be printed. Listing 5-2 expects two non-null command-line arguments and uses this expansion to display error messages when they are missing or null.

Listing 5-2. checkarg, Exit If Parameters Are Unset or Empty

```
## Check for unset arguments
: ${1?An argument is required} \
  ${2?Two arguments are required}

## Check for empty arguments
: ${1:?A non-empty argument is required} \
  ${2:?Two non-empty arguments are required}

echo "Thank you."
```

The message will be printed by the first expansion that fails, and the script will exit at that point:

```
$ checkarg
/home/chris/bin/checkarg: line 10: 1: An argument is required
$ checkarg x
/home/chris/bin/checkarg: line 10: 2: Two arguments are required
$ checkarg '' ''
/home/chris/bin/checkarg: line 13: 1: A non-empty argument is required
$ checkarg x ''
/home/chris/bin/checkarg: line 13: 2: Two non-empty arguments are required
$ checkarg x x
Thank you.
```

POSIX Shell

Besides the expansions from the Bourne shell, the POSIX shell includes a number of expansions from the KornShell. These include returning the length and removing a pattern from the beginning or end of a variable's contents.

${#var}: Length of Variable's Contents

This expansion returns the length of the expanded value of the variable:

```
read passwd
if [ ${#passwd} -lt 8 ]
then
  printf "Password is too short: %d characters\n" "$#" >&2
  exit 1
fi
```

${var%PATTERN}: Remove the Shortest Match from the End

The variable is expanded, and the shortest string that matches PATTERN is removed from the end of the expanded value. The PATTERN here and in other parameter expansions is a filename expansion (aka *file globbing*) pattern.

Given the string Toronto and the pattern o*, the shortest matching pattern is the final o:

```
$ var=Toronto
$ var=${var%o*}
$ printf "%s\n" "$var"
Toront
```

Because the truncated string has been assigned to var, the shortest string that now matches the pattern is ont:

```
$ printf "%s\n" "${var%o*}"
Tor
```

This expansion can be used to replace the external command, dirname, which strips the filename portion of a path, leaving the path to the directory (Listing 5-3). If there is no slash in the string, the current directory is printed if it is the name of an existing file in the current directory; otherwise, a dot is printed.

Listing 5-3. dname, Print the Directory Portion of a File Path

```
case $1 in
  */*) printf "%s\n" "${1%/*}" ;;
  *) [ -e "$1" ] && printf "%s\n" "$PWD" || echo '.' ;;
esac
```

■ **Note** I have called this script dname rather than dirname because it doesn't follow the POSIX specification for the dirname command. In the next chapter, there is a shell function called dirname that does implement the POSIX command.

```
$ dname /etc/passwd
/etc
$ dname bin
/home/chris
```

${var%%PATTERN}: Remove the Longest Match from the End

The variable is expanded, and the longest string that matches PATTERN from the end of the expanded value is removed:

```
$ var=Toronto
$ sa "${var%%o*}"
:t:
```

${var#PATTERN}: Remove the Shortest Match from the Beginning

The variable is expanded, and the shortest string that matches PATTERN is removed from the beginning of the expanded value:

```
$ var=Toronto
$ sa "${var#*o}"
:ronto:
```

${var##PATTERN}: Remove the Longest Match from the Beginning

The variable is expanded, and the longest string that matches PATTERN is removed from the beginning of the expanded value. This is often used to extract the name of a script from the $0 parameter, which contains the full path to the script:

```
scriptname=${0##*/} ## /home/chris/bin/script => script
```

Bash

Two expansions from KornShell 93 were introduced in bash2: search and replace and substring extraction.

${var//PATTERN/STRING}: Replace All Instances of PATTERN with STRING

Because the question mark matches any single character, this example hides a password:

```
$ passwd=zxQ1.=+-a
$ printf "%s\n" "${passwd//?/*}"
*********
```

With a single slash, only the first matching character is replaced.

```
$ printf "%s\n" "${passwd/[[:punct:]]/*}"
zxQ1*=+-a
```

${var:OFFSET:LENGTH}: Return a Substring of $var

A substring of $var starting at OFFSET is returned. If LENGTH is specified, that number of characters is substituted; otherwise, the rest of the string is returned. The first character is at offset 0:

```
$ var=Toronto
$ sa "${var:3:2}"
:on:
$ sa "${var:3}"
:onto:
```

A negative OFFSET is counted from the end of the string. If a literal minus sign is used (as opposed to one contained in a variable), it must be preceded by a space to prevent it from being interpreted as a default expansion:

```
$ sa "${var: -3}"
:nto:
```

${!var}: Indirect Reference

If you have one variable containing the name of another, for example x=yes and a=x, bash can use an indirect reference:

```
$ x=yes
$ a=x
$ sa "${!a}"
:yes:
```

The same effect can be had using the eval builtin command, which expands its arguments and executes the resulting string as a command:

```
$ eval "sa \$$a"
:yes:
```

See Chapter 9 for a more detailed explanation of eval.

Bash-4.0

In version 4.0, bash introduced two new parameter expansions, one for converting to uppercase and one for lowercase. Both have single-character and global versions.

${var^PATTERN}: Convert to Uppercase

The first character of var is converted to uppercase if it matches PATTERN; with a double caret (^^), it converts all characters matching PATTERN. If PATTERN is omitted, all characters are matched:

```
$ var=toronto
$ sa "${var^}"
:Toronto:
$ sa "${var^[n-z]}"
:Toronto:
$ sa "${var^^[a-m]}" ## matches all characters from a to m inclusive
:toronto:
$ sa "${var^^[n-q]}"
:tOrONtO:
$ sa "${var^^}"
:TORONTO:
```

${var,PATTERN}: Convert to Lowercase

This expansion works in the same way as the previous one, except that it converts uppercase to lowercase:

```
$ var=TORONTO
$ sa "${var,,}"
:toronto:
$ sa "${var,,[N-Q]}"
:ToRonTo:
```

Positional Parameters

The positional parameters can be referenced individually by number ($1 … $9 ${10} …) or all at once with "$@" or "$*". As has already been noted, parameters greater than 9 must be enclosed in braces: ${10}, ${11}.

The shift command without an argument removes the first positional parameter and shifts the remaining arguments forward so that $2 becomes $1, $3 becomes $2, and so on. With an argument, it can remove more. To remove the first three parameters, supply an argument with the number of parameters to remove:

```
$ shift 3
```

To remove all the parameters, use the special parameter $#, which contains the number of positional parameters:

```
$ shift "$#"
```

To remove all but the last two positional parameters, use this:

```
$ shift $(( $# - 2 ))
```

To use each parameter in turn, there are two common methods. The first way is to loop through the values of the parameters by expanding "$@":

```
for param in "$@"  ## or just:  for param
do
  : do something with $param
done
```

And this is the second:

```
while [ $# -gt 0 ]  ## or: while [ -n "$*" ]
do
  : do something with $1
  shift
done
```

Arrays

All the variables used so far have been *scalar variables*; that is, they contain only a single value. In contrast, *array variables* can contain many values. The POSIX shell does not support arrays, but bash (since version 2) does. Its arrays are one dimensional and indexed by integers, or, since bash-4.0, with strings.

Integer-Indexed Arrays

The individual members of an array variable are assigned and accessed with a subscript of the form [N]. The first element has an index of 0. In bash, arrays are sparse; they needn't be assigned with consecutive indices. An array can have an element with an index of 0, another with an index of 42, and no intervening elements.

Displaying Arrays

Array elements are referenced by the name and a subscript in braces. This example will use the shell variable BASH_VERSINFO. It is an array that contains version information for the running shell. The first element is the major version number, the second the minor:

```
$ printf "%s\n" "${BASH_VERSINFO[0]}"
4
$ printf "%s\n" "${BASH_VERSINFO[1]}"
0
```

All the elements of an array can be printed with a single statement. The subscripts @ and * are analogous to their use with the positional parameters: * expands to a single parameter if quoted; if unquoted, word splitting and file name expansion is performed on the result. Using @ as the subscript and quoting the expansion, each element expands to a separate argument, and no further expansion is performed on them.

```
$ printf "%s\n" "${BASH_VERSINFO[*]}"
4 0 10 1 release i686-pc-linux-gnuoldld
$  printf "%s\n" "${BASH_VERSINFO[@]}"
4
0
10
1
release
i686-pc-linux-gnuoldld
```

Various parameter expansions work on arrays; for example, to get the second and third elements from an array, use this:

```
$ printf "%s\n" "${BASH_VERSINFO[@]:1:2}" ## minor version number and patch level
0
10
```

The length expansion returns the number of elements in the array when the subscript is * or @, and it returns the length of an individual element if a numeric index is given:

```
$ printf "%s\n" "${#BASH_VERSINFO[*]}"
6
$ printf "%s\n" "${#BASH_VERSINFO[2]}" "${#BASH_VERSINFO[5]}"
2
22
```

Assigning Array Elements

Elements can be assigned using an index; the following commands create a sparse array:

```
name[0]=Aaron
name[42]=Adams
```

Indexed arrays are more useful when elements are assigned consecutively (or *packed*), because it makes operations on them simpler. Assignments can be made directly to the next unassigned element:

```
$ unset a
$ a[${#a[@]}]="1 $RANDOM" ## ${#a[@]} is 0
$ a[${#a[@]}]="2 $RANDOM" ## ${#a[@]} is 1
$ a[${#a[@]}]="3 $RANDOM" ## ${#a[@]} is 2
$ a[${#a[@]}]="4 $RANDOM" ## ${#a[@]} is 3
$ printf "%s\n" "${a[@]}"
1 6007
2 3784
3 32330
4 25914
```

An entire array can be populated with a single command:

```
$ province=( Quebec Ontario Manitoba )
$ printf "%s\n" "${province[@]}"
Quebec
Ontario
Manitoba
```

Starting with bash-3.1, the += operator can be used to append values to the end of an indexed array. This results in a neater form of assignment to the next unassigned element:

```
$ province+=( Saskatchewan )
$ province+=( Alberta "British Columbia" "Nova Scotia" )
$ printf "%-25s %-25s %s\n" "${province[@]}"
Quebec                    Ontario                  Manitoba
Saskatchewan              Alberta                  British Columbia
Nova Scotia
```

Associative Arrays

Associative arrays, introduced in bash in version 4.0, use strings as subscripts and must be declared before being used:

```
$ declare -A array
$ for subscript in a b c d e
> do
>   array[$subscript]="$subscript $RANDOM"
> done
$ printf ":%s:\n" "${array["c"]}" ## print one element
:c 1574:
$ printf ":%s:\n" "${array[@]}" ## print the entire array
:a 13856:
:b 6235:
:c 1574:
:d 14020:
:e 9165:
```

Summary

By far the largest subject in this chapter is parameter expansion, and by far the largest section of parameter expansion is devoted to those expansions that were introduced by the KornShell and incorporated into the standard Unix shell. These are tools that give the POSIX shell much of its power. The examples given in this chapter are relatively simple; the full potential of parameter expansion will be shown as you develop serious programs later in the book.

Next in importance are arrays. Though not part of the POSIX standard, they add a great deal of functionality to the shell by making it possible to collect data in logical units.

Understanding the scope of variables can save a lot of head scratching, and well-named variables make a program more understandable and maintainable.

Manipulating the positional parameters is a minor but important aspect of shell programming, and the examples given in this chapter will be revisited and expanded upon later in the book.

Commands

- declare: Declares variables and sets their attributes

- eval: Expands arguments and executes the resulting command

- export: Places variables into the environment so that they are available to child processes

- shift: Deletes and renumbers positional parameters

- shopt: Sets shell options

- unset: Removes a variable entirely

Concepts

- *Environment:* A collection of variables inherited from the calling program and passed to child processes

- *Array variables:* Variables that contain more than one value and accessed using a subscript

- *Scalar variables:* Variables that contain a single value

- *Associative arrays:* Array variables whose subscript is a string rather than an integer

Exercises

1. By default, where can a variable assigned in a script be accessed? Select all that apply:

   - In the current script

   - In functions defined in the current script

   - In the script that called the current script

   - In scripts called by the current script

   - In subshells of the current script

2. I advise against using single-letter variables names but give a couple of places where they are reasonable. Can you think of any other legitimate uses for them?

3. Given `var=192.168.0.123`, write a script that uses parameter expansion to extract the second number, `168`.

CHAPTER 6

■■■

Shell Functions

A *shell function* is a compound command that has been given a name. It stores a series of commands for later execution. The name becomes a command in its own right and can be used in the same way as any other command. Its arguments are available in the positional parameters, just as in any other script. Like other commands, it sets a return code.

A function is executed in the same process as the script that calls it. This makes it fast, because no new process has to be created. All the variables of the script are available to it without having to be exported, and when a function changes those variables, the changes will be seen by the calling script. That said, you can make variables local to the function so that they do not affect the calling script; the choice is yours.

Not only do functions encapsulate code for reuse in a single script, but they can make it available to other scripts. They make top-down design easy and improve legibility. They break scripts into manageable chunks that can be tested and debugged separately.

At the command line, functions can do things that an external script cannot, such as change directories. They are much more flexible and powerful than aliases, which simply replace the command you type with a different command. Chapter 11 presents a number of functions that make working at the prompt more productive.

Definition Syntax

When shell functions were introduced in the KornShell, the definition syntax was as follows:

```
function name <compound command>
```

When the Bourne shell added functions in 1984, the syntax (which was later included in ksh and adopted by the POSIX standard) was as follows:

```
name() <compound command>
```

Bash allows either syntax as well as the hybrid:

```
function name() <compound command>
```

The following is a function that I wrote several years ago and that, I recently discovered, is included as an example in the bash source code package. It checks whether a dotted-quad Internet Protocol (IP) address is valid. In this book, we always use the POSIX syntax for function definition:

```
isvalidip()
```

Then the body of the function is enclosed in braces ({ ... }) followed by optional redirection (see the uinfo function later in this chapter for an example).

The first set of tests is contained in a case statement:

```
case $1 in
  "" | *[!0-9.]* | *[!0-9]) return 1 ;;
esac
```

It checks for an empty string, invalid characters, or an address that doesn't end with a digit. If any of these items is found, the shell builtin command return is invoked with an exit status of 1. This exits the function and returns control to the calling script. An argument sets the function's return code; if there is no argument, the exit code of the function defaults to that of the last command executed.

The next command, local, is a shell builtin that restricts a variable's scope to the function (and its children), but the variable will not change in the parent process. Setting IFS to a period causes word splitting at periods, rather than whitepace, when a parameter is expanded. Beginning with bash-4.0, local and declare have an option, -A, to declare an associative array.

```
local IFS=.
```

The set builtin replaces the positional parameters with its arguments. Since $IFS is a period, each element of the IP address is assigned to a different parameter.

```
set -- $1
```

The final two lines check each positional parameter in turn. If it's greater than 255, it is not valid in a dotted-quad IP address. If a parameter is empty, it is replaced with the invalid value of 666. If all tests are successful, the function exits successfully; if not, the return code is 1, or failure.

```
[ ${1:-666} -le 255 ] && [ ${2:-666} -le 255 ] &&
[ ${3:-666} -le 255 ] && [ ${4:-666} -le 255 ]
```

Listing 6-1 shows the complete function with comments.

Listing 6-1. isvalidip, Check Argument for Valid Dotted-Quad IP Address

```
isvalidip() #@ USAGE: isvalidip DOTTED-QUAD
{
  case $1 in
    ## reject the following:
    ##    empty string
    ##    anything other than digits and dots
    ##    anything not ending in a digit
    "" | *[!0-9.]* | *[!0-9]) return 1 ;;
  esac

  ## Change IFS to a dot, but only in this function
  local IFS=.
```

```
## Place the IP address into the positional parameters;
## after word splitting each element becomes a parameter
set -- $1

[ $# -eq 4 ] && ## must be four parameters
                ## each must be less than 256
## A default of 666 (which is invalid) is used if a parameter is empty
## All four parameters must pass the test
[ ${1:-666} -le 255 ] && [ ${2:-666} -le 255 ] &&
[ ${3:-666} -le 255 ] && [ ${4:-666} -le 255 ]
}
```

■ **Note** Formats other than dotted quads can be valid IP addresses, as in `127.1`, `216.239.10085`, and `3639551845`.

The function returns successfully (that is, a return code of 0) if the argument supplied on the command line is a valid dotted-quad IP address. You can test the function at the command line by sourcing the file containing the function:

```
$ . isvalidip-func
```

The function is now available at the shell prompt. Let's test it with a few IP addresses:

```
$ for ip in 127.0.0.1 168.260.0.234 1.2.3.4 123.100.34.21 204.225.122.150
> do
>   if isvalidip "$ip"
>   then
>     printf "%15s: valid\n" "$ip"
>   else
>     printf "%15s: invalid\n" "$ip"
>   fi
> done
        127.0.0.1: valid
  168.260.0.234: invalid
          1.2.3.4: valid
  123.100.34.21: invalid
204.225.122.150: valid
```

Compound Commands

A *compound command* is a list of commands enclosed in (…) or { … }, expressions enclosed in ((…)) or [[…]], or one of the block-level shell keywords (that is, case, for, select, while, and until).

The valint program from Chapter 3 is a good candidate for converting to a function. It is likely to be called more than once, so the time saved could be significant. The program is a single compound command, so braces are not necessary (see Listing 6-2).

Listing 6-2. valint, Check for Valid Integer

```
valint() #@ USAGE: valint INTEGER
  case ${1#-} in        ## Leading hyphen removed to accept negative numbers
    *[!0-9]*) false;; ## the string contains a non-digit character
    *) true ;;          ## the whole number, and nothing but the number
  esac
```

If a function's body is wrapped in parentheses, then it is executed in a subshell, and changes made during its execution do not remain in effect after it exits:

```
$ funky() ( name=nobody; echo "name = $name" )
$ name=Rumpelstiltskin
$ funky
name = nobody
$ echo "name = $name"
name = Rumpelstiltskin
```

Getting Results

The two previous functions are both called for their exit status; the calling program needs to know only whether the function succeeds or fails. Functions can also return information from a range of return codes, by setting one or more variables or by printing its results.

Set Different Exit Codes

You can convert the rangecheck script from Chapter 3 to a function with a couple of improvements; it returns 0 on success as before but differentiates between a number that is too high and one that is too low. It returns 1 if the number is too low, or it returns 2 if it is too high. It also accepts the range to be checked as arguments on the command line, defaulting to 10 and 20 if no range is given (Listing 6-3).

Listing 6-3. rangecheck, Check Whether an Integer Is Within a Specified Range

```
rangecheck() #@ USAGE: rangecheck int [low [high]]
  if [ "$1" -lt ${2:-10} ]
  then
    return 1
  elif [ "$1" -gt ${3:-20} ]
  then
    return 2
  else
    return 0
  fi
```

Return codes are a single, unsigned byte; therefore, their range is 0 to 255. If you need numbers larger than 255 or less than 0, use one of the other methods of returning a value.

Print the Result

A function's purpose may be to print information, either to the terminal or to a file (Listing 6-4).

Listing 6-4. uinfo, Print Information About the Environment

```
uinfo() #@ USAGE: uinfo [file]
{
  printf "%12s: %s\n" \
    USER    "${USER:-No value assigned}" \
    PWD     "${PWD:-No value assigned}" \
    COLUMNS "${COLUMNS:-No value assigned}" \
    LINES   "${LINES:-No value assigned}" \
    SHELL   "${SHELL:-No value assigned}" \
    HOME    "${HOME:-No value assigned}" \
    TERM    "${TERM:-No value assigned}"
} > ${1:-/dev/fd/1}
```

The redirection is evaluated at runtime. In this example, it expands to the function's first argument or to /dev/fd/1 (standard output) if no argument is given:

```
$ uinfo
        USER: chris
         PWD: /home/chris/work/BashProgramming
     COLUMNS: 100
       LINES: 43
       SHELL: /bin/bash
        HOME: /home/chris
        TERM: rxvt
$ cd; uinfo $HOME/tmp/info
$ cat $HOME/tmp/info
        USER: chris
         PWD: /home/chris
     COLUMNS: 100
       LINES: 43
       SHELL: /bin/bash
        HOME: /home/chris
            TERM: rxvt
```

When the output is printed to the standard output, it may be captured using command substitution:

```
info=$( uinfo )
```

But command substitution creates a new process and is therefore slow; save it for use with external commands. When a script needs output from a function, put it into variables.

Place Results in One or More Variables

I was writing a script that needed to sort three integers from lowest to highest. I didn't want to call an external command for a maximum of three comparisons, so I wrote the function shown in Listing 6-5. It stores the results in three variables: _MIN3, _MID3, and _MAX3.

Listing 6-5. _max3, Sort Three Integers

```
_max3() { #@ Sort 3 integers and store in $_MAX3, $_MID3 and $_MIN3
    [ $# -ne 3  ] && return 5
    [ $1 -gt $2 ] && { set -- $2 $1 $3; }
    [ $2 -gt $3 ] && { set -- $1 $3 $2; }
    [ $1 -gt $2 ] && { set -- $2 $1 $3; }
    _MAX3=$3
    _MID3=$2
    _MIN3=$1
}
```

I use the convention of beginning function names with an underscore when they set a variable rather than print the result. The variable is the name of the function converted to uppercase. In this instance, I needed two other variables as well.

Function Libraries

In my `scripts` directory, I have about 100 files of nothing but functions. A few contain only a single function, but most are collections of functions with a common theme. Sourcing one of these files defines a number of related functions that can be used in the current script.

I have a library of functions for manipulating dates and another for dissecting strings. I have one for creating PostScript files of chess diagrams and one for playing with crossword puzzles. There's a library for reading function keys and cursor keys and a different one for mouse buttons.

Using Functions from Libraries

Most of the time, I source the library to include all its functions in my script:

```
. date-funcs ## get date-funcs from:
             ## http://cfaj.freeshell.org/shell/ssr/08-The-Dating-Game.shtml
```

Occasionally, I need only one function from a library, so I cut and paste it into the new script.

Sample Script

The following script defines four functions: `die`, `usage`, `version`, and `readline`. The `readline` function will differ according to which shell you are using. The script creates a basic web page, complete with title and primary headline (`<H1>`). The `readline` function uses options to the builtin command `read` that will be examined in detail in Chapter 9.

```
##
## Set defaults
##
prompt=" ==> "
template='<!DOCTYPE html PUBLIC "-//W3C//DTD HTML 4.01//EN"
         "http://www.w3.org/TR/html4/strict.dtd">
```

```
<html lang="en">
  <head>
    <title>%s</title>
    <link href="%s" rel="stylesheet" type="text/css">
  </head>
  <body>
    <h1>%s</h1>
    <div id="main">

    </div>
  </body>
</html>
'


##
## Define shell functions
##
die() ## DESCRIPTION: Print error message and exit with ERRNO code
{ ## USAGE: die ERRNO MESSAGE ...
  error=$1
  shift
  [ -n "$*" ] && printf "%s\n" "$*" >&2
  exit "$error"
}

usage()
{
  printf "USAGE: %s HTMLFILE\n" "$progname"
}

version()
{
  printf "%s version %s" "$progname" "${version:-1}"
}

#@ USAGE: readline var prompt default
#@ DESCRIPTION: Prompt user for string and offer default
##
#@ Define correct version for your version of bash or other shell
bashversion=${BASH_VERSION%%.*}
if [ ${bashversion:-0} -ge 4 ]
then
  ## bash4.0 has an -i option for editing a supplied value
  readline()
  {
    read -ep "${2:-"$prompt"}" -i "$3" "$1"
  }
elif [ ${BASHVERSION:-0} -ge 2 ]
then
  readline()
  {
    history -s "$3"
```

```
    printf "Press up arrow to edit default value: '%s'\n" "${3:-none}"
    read -ep "${2:-"$prompt"}" "$1"
  }
else
  readline()
  {
    printf "Press enter for default of '%s'\n" "$3"
    printf "%s " "${2:-"$prompt"}"
    read
    eval "$1=\${REPLY:-"$3"}"
  }
fi

if [ $# -ne 1 ]
then
  usage
  exit 1
fi

filename=$1

readline title "Page title: "
readline h1 "Main headline: " "$title"
readline css "Style sheet file: " "${filename%.*}.css"

printf "$template" "$title" "$css" "$h1" > "$filename"
```

Summary

Shell functions enable you to create large, fast, sophisticated programs. Without them, the shell could hardly be called a real programming language. Functions will be part of almost everything from here to the end of the book.

Commands

- `local`: Restricts a variable's scope to the current function and its children

- `return`: Exits a function (with an optional return code)

- `set`: With --, replaces the positional parameters with the remaining arguments (after --)

Exercises

1. Rewrite function isvalidip using parameter expansion instead of changing IFS.

2. Add a check to _max3 to verify that all three arguments are integers.

CHAPTER 7

■ ■ ■

String Manipulation

In the Bourne shell, very little string manipulation was possible without resorting to external commands. Strings could be concatenated by juxtaposition, they could be split by changing the value of IFS, and they could be searched with case, but anything else required an external command.

Even things that *could* be done entirely in the shell were often relegated to external commands, and that practice has continued to this day. In some current Linux distributions, you can find the following snippet in /etc/profile. It checks whether a directory is included in the PATH variable:

```
if ! echo ${PATH} |grep -q /usr/games
then
  PATH=$PATH:/usr/games
fi
```

Even in a Bourne shell, you can do this without an external command:

```
case :$PATH: in
  *:/usr/games:*);;
  *) PATH=$PATH:/usr/games ;;
esac
```

The POSIX shell includes a number of parameter expansions that slice and dice strings, and bash adds even more. These were outlined in Chapter 5, and their use is expanded upon in this chapter along with other string techniques.

Concatenation

Concatenation is the joining together of two or more items to form one larger item. In this case, the items are strings. They are joined by placing one after the other. A common example, which I used in Chapter 1, adds a directory to the PATH variable. It concatenates a variable with a single-character string (:), another variable, and a literal string:

```
PATH=$PATH:$HOME/bin
```

If the right side of the assignment contains a literal space or other character special to the shell, then it must be quoted with double quotes (variables inside single quotes are not expanded):

```
var=$HOME/bin # this comment is not part of the assignment
var="$HOME/bin # but this is"
```

In bash-3.1, a string append operator (+=) was added:

```
$ var=abc
$ var+=xyz
$ echo "$var"
abcxyz
```

Because this offers very little advantage over the standard method (var=${var}xyz), there is no good reason to use it. (It does make sense to use += for appending to an array, as demonstrated in Chapter 5.)

Repeat Character to a Given Length

Concatenation is used in this function that builds a string of N characters; it loops, adding one instance of $1 each time, until the string ($_REPEAT) reaches the desired length (contained in $2).

```
_repeat()
{
  #@ USAGE: _repeat string number
  _REPEAT=
  while [ ${#_REPEAT} -lt $2 ]
  do
    _REPEAT=$_REPEAT$1
  done
}
```

The result is stored in the variable _REPEAT:

```
$ _repeat % 40
$ printf "%s\n" "$_REPEAT"
%%%%%%%%%%%%%%%%%%%%%%%%%%%%%%%%%%%%%%%%%%
```

You can speed that function up by concatenating more than one instance in each loop so that the length increases geometrically. The problem with this version is that the resulting string will usually be longer than required. To fix that, parameter expansion is used to trim the string to the desired length (Listing 7-1).

Listing 7-1. repeat, Repeat a String N Times

```
_repeat()
{
  #@ USAGE: _repeat string number
  _REPEAT=$1
  while [ ${#_REPEAT} -lt $2 ] ## Loop until string exceeds desired length
  do
    _REPEAT=$_REPEAT$_REPEAT$_REPEAT ## 3 seems to be the optimum number
  done
  _REPEAT=${_REPEAT:0:$2} ## Trim to desired length
}

repeat()
{
```

```
  _repeat "$@"
  printf "%s\n" "$_REPEAT"
}
```

The _repeat function is called by the alert function (Listing 7-2).

Listing 7-2. alert, Print a Warning Message with a Border and a Beep

```
alert() #@ USAGE: alert message border
{
  _repeat "${2:-#}" $(( ${#1} + 8 ))
  printf '\a%s\n' "$_REPEAT" ## \a = BEL
  printf '%2.2s  %s  %2.2s\n' "$_REPEAT" "$1" "$_REPEAT"
  printf '%s\n' "$_REPEAT"
}
```

The function prints the message surrounded by a border generated with _repeat:

```
$ alert "Do you really want to delete all your files?"
##################################################
##  Do you really want to delete all your files?  ##
##################################################
```

The border character can be changed with a command-line argument:

```
$ alert "Danger, Will Robinson" $
$$$$$$$$$$$$$$$$$$$$$$$$$$$$$$$$$
$$  Danger, Will Robinson  $$
$$$$$$$$$$$$$$$$$$$$$$$$$$$$$$$$$
```

Processing Character by Character

There are no direct parameter expansions to give either the first or last character of a string, but by using the wildcard (?), a string can be expanded to everything *except* its first or last character:

```
$ var=strip
$ allbutfirst=${var#?}
$ allbutlast=${var%?}
$ sa "$allbutfirst" "$allbutlast"
:trip:
:stri:
```

The values of allbutfirst and allbutlast can then be removed from the original variable to give the first or last character:

```
$ first=${var%"$allbutfirst"}
$ last=${var#"$allbutlast"}
$ sa "$first" "$last"
:s:
:p:
```

The first character of a string can also be obtained with printf:

```
printf -v first "%c" "$var"
```

To operate on each character of a string one at a time, use a while loop and a temporary variable that stores the value of var minus its first character. The temp variable is then used as the pattern in a ${var%PATTERN} expansion. Finally, $temp is assigned to var, and the loop continues until there are no characters left in var:

```
while [ -n "$var" ]
do
  temp=${var#?}          ## everything but the first character
  char=${var%"$temp"}   ## remove everything but the first character
  : do something with "$char"
  var=$temp              ## assign truncated value to var
done
```

Reversal

You can use the same method to reverse the order of characters in a string. Each letter is tacked on to the end of a new variable (Listing 7-3).

Listing 7-3. revstr, Reverse the Order of a String; Store Result in _REVSTR

```
_revstr() #@ USAGE: revstr STRING
{
  var=$1
  _REVSTR=
  while [ -n "$var" ]
  do
    temp=${var#?}
    _REVSTR=$temp${var%"$temp"}
    var=$temp
  done
}
```

Case Conversion

In the Bourne shell, case conversion was done with external commands such as tr, which translates characters in its first argument to the corresponding character in its second argument:

```
$ echo abcdefgh | tr ceh CEH # c => C, e => E, h => H
abCdEfgH
$ echo abcdefgh | tr ceh HEC # c => H, e => E, h => C
abHdEfgC
```

Ranges specified with a hyphen are expanded to include all intervening characters:

```
$ echo touchdown | tr 'a-z' 'A-Z'
TOUCHDOWN
```

In the POSIX shell, short strings can be converted efficiently using parameter expansion and a function containing a case statement as a lookup table. The function looks up the first character of its first argument and stores the uppercase equivalent in _UPR. If the first character is not a lowercase letter, it is unchanged (Listing 7-4).

Listing 7-4. to_upper, Convert First Character of $1 to Uppercase

```
to_upper()
    case $1 in
        a*) _UPR=A ;; b*) _UPR=B ;; c*) _UPR=C ;; d*) _UPR=D ;;
        e*) _UPR=E ;; f*) _UPR=F ;; g*) _UPR=G ;; h*) _UPR=H ;;
        i*) _UPR=I ;; j*) _UPR=J ;; k*) _UPR=K ;; l*) _UPR=L ;;
        m*) _UPR=M ;; n*) _UPR=N ;; o*) _UPR=O ;; p*) _UPR=P ;;
        q*) _UPR=Q ;; r*) _UPR=R ;; s*) _UPR=S ;; t*) _UPR=T ;;
        u*) _UPR=U ;; v*) _UPR=V ;; w*) _UPR=W ;; x*) _UPR=X ;;
        y*) _UPR=Y ;; z*) _UPR=Z ;;  *) _UPR=${1%${1#?}} ;;
    esac
```

To capitalize a word (that is, just the first letter), call to_upper with the word as an argument, and append the rest of the word to $_UPR:

```
$ word=function
$ to_upper "$word"
$ printf "%c%s\n" "$_UPR" "${word#?}"
Function
```

To convert the entire word to uppercase, you can use the upword function shown in Listing 7-5.

Listing 7-5. upword, Convert Word to Uppercase

```
_upword() #@ USAGE: upword STRING
{
  local word=$1
  while [ -n "$word" ] ## loop until nothing is left in $word
  do
    to_upper "$word"
    _UPWORD=$_UPWORD$_UPR
    word=${word#?} ## remove the first character from $word
  done
}

upword()
{
  _upword "$@"
  printf "%s\n" "$_UPWORD"
}
```

You can use the same technique to convert uppercase to lowercase, but I'll leave the coding of that as an exercise for you.

The basics of case conversion using the parameter expansions introduced in bash-4.0 were covered in Chapter 5. Some uses for them are shown in the following sections.

Comparing Contents Without Regard to Case

When getting user input, a programmer often wants to accept it in either uppercase or lowercase or even a mixture of the two. When the input is a single letter, as in asking for Y or N, the code is simple. There is a choice of using the or symbol (|):

```
read ok
case $ok in
  y|Y) echo "Great!" ;;
  n|N) echo Good-bye
       exit 1
    ;;
  *) echo Invalid entry ;;
esac
```

or a bracketed character list:

```
read ok
case $ok in
  [yY]) echo "Great!" ;;
  [nN]) echo Good-bye
       exit 1
    ;;
  *) echo Invalid entry ;;
esac
```

When the input is longer, the first method requires all possible combinations to be listed, for example:

```
jan | jaN | jAn | jAN | Jan | JaN | JAn | JAN) echo "Great!" ;;
```

The second method works but is ugly and hard to read, and the longer the string is, the harder and uglier it gets:

```
read monthname
case $monthname in ## convert $monthname to number
  [Jj][Aa][Nn]*) month=1 ;;
  [Ff][Ee][Bb]*) month=2 ;;
  ## ...put the rest of the year here
  [Dd][Ee][Cc]*) month=12 ;;
  [1-9]|1[0-2]) month=$monthname ;; ## accept number if entered
  *) echo "Invalid month: $monthname" >&2 ;;
esac
```

A better solution is to convert the input to uppercase first and then compare it:

```
_upword "$monthname"
case $_UPWORD in ## convert $monthname to number
  JAN*) month=1 ;;
  FEB*) month=2 ;;
  ## ...put the rest of the year here
```

```
    DEC*) month=12 ;;
    [1-9]|1[0-2]) month=$monthname ;; ## accept number if entered
    *) echo "Invalid month: $monthname" >&2 ;;
esac
```

■ **Note** See Listing 7-11 at the end of this chapter for another method of converting a month name to a number.

In bash-4.0, you can replace the _upword function with case ${monthname^^} in, although I might keep it in a function to ease transition between versions of bash:

```
_upword()
{
   _UPWORD=${1^^}
}
```

Check for Valid Variable Name

You and I know what constitutes a valid variable name, but do your users? If you ask a user to enter a variable name, as you might in a script that creates other scripts, you should check that what is entered is a valid name. The function to do that is a simple check for violation of the rules: a name must contain only letters, numbers, and underscores and must begin with a letter or an underscore (Listing 7-6).

Listing 7-6. validname, Check $1 for a Valid Variable or Function Name

```
validname() #@ USAGE: validname varname
 case $1 in
    ## doesn't begin with letter or underscore, or
    ## contains something not letter, number, or underscore
    [!a-zA-Z_]* | *[!a-zA-z0-9_]* ) return 1;;
 esac
```

The function is successful if the first argument is a valid variable name; otherwise, it fails.

```
$ for name in name1 2var first.name first_name last-name
> do
>    validname "$name" && echo "  valid: $name" || echo "invalid: $name"
> done
  valid: name1
invalid: 2var
invalid: first.name
  valid: first_name
invalid: last-name
```

Insert One String into Another

To insert a string into another string, it is necessary to split the string into two parts—the part that will be to the left of the inserted string and the part to the right. Then the insertion string is sandwiched between them.

   This function takes three arguments: the main string, the string to be inserted, and the position at which to insert it. If the position is omitted, it defaults to inserting after the first character. The work is done by the first function, which stores the result in _insert_string. This function can be called to save the cost of using command substitution. The insert_string function takes the same arguments, which it passes to _insert_string and then prints the result (Listing 7-7).

Listing 7-7. insert_string, Insert One String into Another at a Specified Location

```
_insert_string() #@ USAGE: _insert_string STRING INSERTION [POSITION]
{
  local insert_string_dflt=2              ## default insert location
  local string=$1                         ## container string
  local i_string=$2                       ## string to be inserted
  local i_pos=${3:-${insert_string_dflt:-2}} ## insert location
  local left right                        ## before and after strings
  left=${string:0:$(( $i_pos - 1 ))}      ## string to left of insert
  right=${string:$(( $i_pos - 1 ))}       ## string to right of insert
  _insert_string=$left$i_string$right     ## build new string
}

insert_string()
{
  _insert_string "$@" && printf "%s\n" "$_insert_string"
}
```

Examples

```
$ insert_string poplar u 4
popular
$ insert_string show ad 3
shadow
$ insert_string tail ops  ## use default position
topsail
```

Overlay

To overlay a string on top of another string, the technique is similar to inserting a string, the difference being that the right side of the string begins not immediately after the left side but at the length of the overlay further along (Listing 7-8).

Listing 7-8. overlay, Place One String Over the Top of Another

```
_overlay() #@ USAGE: _overlay STRING SUBSTRING START
{          #@ RESULT: in $_OVERLAY
  local string=$1
  local sub=$2
  local start=$3
  local left right
  left=${string:0:start-1}          ## See note below
  right=${string:start+${#sub}-1}
  _OVERLAY=$left$sub$right
}

overlay() #@ USAGE: overlay STRING SUBSTRING START
{
  _overlay "$@" && printf "%s\n" "$_OVERLAY"
}
```

■ **Note** The arithmetic within the substring expansion doesn't need the full POSIX arithmetic syntax; bash will evaluate an expression if it finds one in the place of an integer.

Examples

```
$ {
> overlay pony b 1
> overlay pony u 2
> overlay pony s 3
> overlay pony d 4
> }
bony
puny
posy
pond
```

Trim Unwanted Characters

Variables often arrive with unwanted padding, usually spaces or leading zeroes. These can easily be removed with a loop and a case statement:

```
var="      John      "
while :    ## infinite loop
do
  case $var in
      ' '*) var=${var#?} ;; ## if $var begins with a space remove it
      *' ') var=${var%?} ;; ## if $var ends with a space remove it
```

```
      *) break ;; ## no more leading or trailing spaces, so exit the loop
  esac
done
```

A faster method finds the longest string that doesn't begin or end with the character to be trimmed and then removes everything but that from the original string. This is similar to getting the first or last character from a string, where we used allbutfirst and allbutlast variables.

If the string is " John ", the longest string that ends in a character that is not to be trimmed is " John". That is removed, and the spaces at the end are stored in rightspaces with this:

```
rightspaces=${var##*[! ]} ## remove everything up to the last non-space
```

Then you remove $rightspaces from $var:

```
var=${var%"$rightspaces"} ## $var now contains "     John"
```

Next, you find all the spaces on the left with this:

```
leftspaces=${var%%[! ]*} ## remove from the first non-space to the end
```

Remove $leftspaces from $var:

```
var=${var#"$leftspaces"} ## $var now contains "John"
```

This technique is refined a little for the trim function (Listing 7-9). Its first argument is the string to be trimmed. If there is a second argument, that is the character that will be trimmed from the string. If no character is supplied, it defaults to a space.

Listing 7-9. trim, Trim Unwanted Characters

```
_trim() #@ Trim spaces (or character in $2) from $1
{
  local trim_string
  _TRIM=$1
  trim_string=${_TRIM##*[!${2:- }]}
  _TRIM=${_TRIM%"$trim_string"}
  trim_string=${_TRIM%%[!${2:- }]*}
  _TRIM=${_TRIM#"$trim_string"}
}

trim() #@ Trim spaces (or character in $2) from $1 and print the result
{
  _trim "$@" && printf "%s\n" "$_TRIM"
}
```

Examples

```
$ trim "  S p a c e d   o u t   "
S p a c e d   o u t
$ trim "0002367.45000" 0
2367.45
```

Index

I wrote the index function to convert a month name into its ordinal number; it returns the position of one string inside another (Listing 7-10). It uses parameter expansion to extract the string that precedes the substring. The index of the substring is one more than the length of the extracted string.

Listing 7-10. index, Return Position of One String Inside Another

```
_index() #@ Store position of $2 in $1 in $_INDEX
{
  local idx
  case $1 in
    "") _INDEX=0; return 1 ;;
    *"$2"*) ## extract up to beginning of the matching portion
            idx=${1%%"$2"*}
            ## the starting position is one more than the length
            _INDEX=$(( ${#idx} + 1 )) ;;
    *) _INDEX=0; return 1 ;;
  esac
}

index()
{
  _index "$@"
  printf "%d\n" "$_INDEX"
}
```

Listing 7-11 shows the function to convert a month name to a number. It converts the first three letters of the month name to uppercase and finds its position in the months string. It divides that position by 4 and adds 1 to get the month number.

Listing 7-11. month2num, Convert a Month Name to Its Ordinal Number

```
_month2num()
{
  local months=JAN.FEB.MAR.APR.MAY.JUN.JUL.AUG.SEP.OCT.NOV.DEC
  _upword "${1:0:3}" ## take first three letters of $1 and convert to uppercase
  _index "$months" "$_UPWORD" || return 1
  _MONTH2NUM=$(( $_INDEX / 4 + 1 ))
}

month2num()
{
  _month2num "$@" &&
  printf "%s\n" "$_MONTH2NUM"
}
```

Summary

You learned the following commands and functions in this chapter.

Commands

- `tr`: Translates characters

Functions

- `repeat`: Repeats a string until it has length N
- `alert`: Prints a warning message with a border and a beep
- `revstr`: Reverses the order of a string; stores result in _REVSTR
- `to_upper`: Converts the first character of $1 to uppercase
- `upword`: Converts a word to uppercase
- `validname`: Checks $1 for a valid variable or function name
- `insert_string`: Inserts one string into another at a specified location
- `overlay`: Places one string over the top of another
- `trim`: Trims unwanted characters
- `index`: Returns the position of one string inside another
- `month2num`: Converts a month name to its ordinal number

Exercises

1. What is wrong with this code (besides the inefficiency noted at the beginning of the chapter)?

   ```
   if ! echo ${PATH} |grep -q /usr/games
     PATH=$PATH:/usr/games
   fi
   ```

2. Write a function called `to_lower` that does the opposite of the `to_upper` function in Listing 7-4.

3. Write a function, `palindrome`, that checks whether its command-line argument is a palindrome (that is, a word or phrase that is spelled the same backward and forward). Note that spaces and punctuation are ignored in the test. Exit successfully if it is a palindrome. Include an option to print a message as well as set the return code.

4. Write two functions, `ltrim` and `rtrim`, that trim characters in the same manner as `trim` but from only one side of the string, left and right, respectively.

CHAPTER 8

∎ ∎ ∎

File Operations and Commands

Because the shell is an interpreted language, it is comparatively slow. Many operations on files are best done with external commands that implicitly loop over the lines of a file. At other times, the shell itself is more efficient. This chapter looks at how the shell works with files—both shell options that modify and extend file name expansion and shell options that read and modify the contents of files. Several external commands that work on files are explained, often accompanied by examples of when *not* to use them.

Some of the scripts in this chapter use an especially prepared file containing the King James version of the Bible. The file can be downloaded from http://cfaj.freeshell.org/kjv/kjv.txt. Download it to your home directory with wget:

```
wget http://cfaj.freeshell.org/kjv/kjv.txt
```

In this file, each verse of the bible is on a single line preceded by the name of the book and the chapter and verse numbers, all delimited with colons:

```
Genesis:001:001:In the beginning God created the heaven and the earth.
Exodus:020:013:Thou shalt not kill.
Exodus:022:018:Thou shalt not suffer a witch to live.
John:011:035:Jesus wept.
```

The path to the file will be kept in the variable kjv, which will be used whenever the file is needed.

```
export kjv=$HOME/kjv.txt
```

Reading a File

The most basic method of reading the contents of a file is a while loop with its input redirected:

```
while read  ## no name supplied so the variable REPLY is used
do
  : do something with "$REPLY" here
done < "$kjv"
```

The file will be stored, one line at a time, in the variable REPLY. More commonly, one or more variable names will be supplied as arguments to read:

```
while read name phone
do
  printf "Name: %-10s\tPhone: %s\n" "$name" "$phone"
done < "$file"
```

The lines are split using the characters in IFS as word delimiters. If the file contained in $file contains these two lines:

```
John 555-1234
Jane 555-7531
```

the output of the previous snippet will be as follows:

```
Name: John      Phone: 555-1234
Name: Jane      Phone: 555-7531
```

By changing the value of IFS before the read command, other characters can be used for word splitting. The same script, using only a hyphen in IFS instead of the default space, tab, and newline, would produce this:

```
$ while IFS=- read name phone
> do
>  printf "Name: %-10s\tPhone: %s\n" "$name" "$phone"
> done < "$file"
Name: John 555  Phone: 1234
Name: Jane 555  Phone: 7531
```

Placing an assignment in front of a command causes it to be local to that command and does not change its value elsewhere in the script.

To read the King James version of the Bible (henceforth referred to as KJV), the field separator IFS should be set to a colon so that lines can be split into book, chapter, verse, and text, each being assigned to a separate variable (Listing 8-1).

Listing 8-1. kjvfirsts, Print Book, Chapter, Verse, and First Words from KJV

```
while IFS=: read book chapter verse text
do
    firstword=${text%% *}
    printf "%s %s:%s %s\n" "$book" "$chapter" "$verse" "$firstword"
done < "$kjv"
```

The output (with more than 31,000 lines replaced by a single ellipsis) looks like this:

```
Genesis 001:001 In
Genesis 001:002 And
Genesis 001:003 And
...
Revelation 022:019 And
Revelation 022:020 He
Revelation 022:021 The
```

On my computer, a 1.6GHz Pentium 4 with many applications running, this script takes more than half a minute to run. The same task written in awk takes about a quarter of the time. See the section on awk later in this chapter for the script.

The awk programming language is often used in shell scripts when the shell itself is too slow (as in this case) or when features not present in the shell are required (for example, arithmetic using decimal fractions). The language is explained in somewhat more detail in the following section.

External Commands

You can accomplish many tasks using the shell without calling any external commands. Some use one or more commands to provide data for a script to process. Other scripts are best written with nothing but external commands.

Often, the functionality of an external command can be duplicated within the shell, and sometimes it cannot. Sometimes using the shell is the most efficient method; sometimes it is the slowest. Here I'll cover a number of external commands that process files and show how they are used (and often misused). These are not detailed explanations of the commands; usually they are an overview with, in most cases, a look at how they are used—or misused—in shell scripts.

cat

One of the most misused commands, cat reads all the files on its command line and prints their contents to the standard output. If no file names are supplied, cat reads the standard input. It is an appropriate command when more than one file needs to be read or when a file needs to be included with the output of other commands:

```
cat *.txt | tr aeiou AEIOU > upvowel.txt

{
  date                ## Print the date and time
  cat report.txt      ## Print the contents of the file
  printf "Signed: "   ## Print "Signed: " without a newline
  whoami              ## Print the user's login name
} | mail -s "Here is the report" paradigm@example.com
```

It is not necessary when the file or files could have been placed on the command line:

```
cat thisfile.txt | head -n 25 > thatfile.txt  ## WRONG
head -n 25 thisfile.txt > thatfile.txt         ## CORRECT
```

It *is* useful when more than one file (or none) needs to be supplied to a command that cannot take a file name as an argument or can take only a single file, as in redirection. It is useful when one or more file names may or may not be on the command line. If no files are given, the standard input is used:

```
cat "$@" | while read x; do whatever; done
```

The same thing can be done using process substitution, the advantage being that variables modified within the while loop will be visible to the rest of the script. The disadvantage is that it makes the script less portable.

```
while read x; do : whatever; done < <( cat "$@" )
```

Another frequent misuse of cat is to use the output as a list with for:

```
for line in $( cat "$kjv" ); do n=$(( ${n:-0} + 1 )); done
```

That script does not put lines into the line variable; it reads each word into it. The value of n will be 795989, which is the number of words in the file. There are 31,102 lines in the file. (And if you really wanted that information, you would use the wc command.)

head

By default, head prints the first ten lines of each file on the command line, or from the standard input if no file name is given. The -n option changes that default:

```
$ head -n 1 "$kjv"
Genesis:001:001:In the beginning God created the heaven and the earth.
```

The output of head, like that of any command, can be stored in a variable:

```
filetop=$( head -n 1 "$kjv")
```

In that instance, head is unnecessary; this shell one-liner does the same thing without any external command:

```
read filetop < "$kjv"
```

Using head to read one line is especially inefficient when the variable then has to be split into its constituent parts:

```
book=${filetop%%:*}
text=${filetop##*:}
```

That can be accomplished much more rapidly with read:

```
$ IFS=: read book chapter verse text < "$kjv"
$ sa "$book" "$chapter" "$verse" "${text%% *}"
:Genesis:
:001:
:001:
:In:
```

Even reading multiple lines into variables can be faster using the shell instead of head:

```
{
  read line1
  read line2
  read line3
  read line4
} < "$kjv"
```

or, you can put the lines into an array:

```
for n in {1..4}
do
  read lines[${#lines[@]}]
done < "$kjv"
```

In bash-4.0, the new builtin command mapfile can also be used to populate an array:

```
mapfile -tn 4 lines < "$kjv"
```

The mapfile command is explained in more detail in Chapter 13.

touch

The default action of touch is to update the timestamp of a file to the current time, creating an empty file if it doesn't exist. An argument to the -d option changes the timestamp to that time rather than the present. It is not necessary to use touch to create a file. The shell can do it with redirection:

```
> filename
```

Even to create multiple files, the shell is faster:

```
for file in {a..z}$RANDOM
do
  > "$file"
done
```

ls

Unless used with one or more options, the ls command offers little functional advantage over shell file name expansion. Both list files in alphabetical order. If you want the files displayed in neat columns across the screen, ls is useful. If you want to do anything with those file names, it can be done better, and often more safely, in the shell.

With options, however, it's a different matter. The -l option prints more information about the file, including its permissions, owner, size, and date of modification. The -t option sorts the files by last modification time, most recent first. The order (whether by name or by time) is reversed with the -r option.

I often see ls misused in a manner that can break a script. File names containing spaces are an abomination, but they are so common nowadays that scripts *must* take their possibility (or should I say inevitability?) into account. In the following construction (that I see all too often), not only is ls unnecessary, but its use will break the script if any file names contain spaces:

```
for file in $(ls); do
```

The result of command substitution is subject to word splitting, so file will be assigned to each word in a file name if it contains spaces:

```
$ touch {zzz,xxx,yyy}\ a  ## create 3 files with a space in their names
$ for file in $(ls *\ *); do echo "$file"; done
xxx
```

```
a
yyy
a
zzz
a
```

On the other hand, using file name expansion gives the desired (that is, correct) results:

```
$ for file in *\ *; do echo "$file"; done
xxx a
yyy a
zzz a
```

cut

The cut command extracts portions of a line, specified either by character or by field. Cut reads from files listed on the command line or from the standard input if no files are specified. The selection to be printed is done by using one of three options, -b, -c, and -f, which stand for bytes, characters, and fields. Bytes and characters differ only when used in locales with multibyte characters. Fields are delimited by a single tab (consecutive tabs delimit empty fields), but that can be changed with the -d option.

The -c option is followed by one or more character positions. Multiple columns (or fields when the -f option is used) can be expressed by a comma-separated list or by a range:

```
$ cut -c 22 "$kjv" | head -n3
e
h
o
$ cut -c 22,24,26 "$kjv" | head -n3
ebg
h a
o a
$ cut -c 22-26 "$kjv" | head -n3
e beg
he ea
od sa
```

A frequent misuse of cut is to extract a portion of a string. Such manipulations can be done with shell parameter expansion. Even if it takes two or three steps, it will be much faster than calling an external command.

```
$ boys="Brian,Carl,Dennis,Mike,Al"
$ printf "%s\n" "$boys" | cut -d, -f3  ## WRONG
Dennis
$ IFS=,            ## Better, no external command used
$ boyarray=( $boys )
$ printf "%s\n" "${boyarray[2]}"
Dennis
$ temp=${boys#*,*,} ## Better still, and more portable
$ printf "%s\n" "${temp%%,*}"
Dennis
```

WC

To count the number of lines, words, or bytes in a file, use wc. By default, it prints all three pieces of information in that order followed by the name of the file. If multiple file names are given on the command line, it prints a line of information for each one and then the total:

```
$ wc "$kjv" /etc/passwd
  31102   795989 4639798 /home/chris/kjv.txt
     50      124    2409 /etc/passwd
  31152   796113 4642207 total
```

If there are no files on the command line, cut reads from the standard input:

```
$ wc < "$kjv"
  31102   795989 4639798
```

The output can be limited to one or two pieces of information by using the -c, -w, or -l option. If any options are used, wc prints only the information requested:

```
$ wc -l "$kjv"
31102 /home/chris/kjv.txt
```

Newer versions of wc have another option, -m, which prints the number of characters, which will be less than the number of bytes if the file contains multibyte characters. The default output remains the same, however.

As with so many commands, wc is often misused to get information about a string rather than a file. To get the length of a string held in a variable, use parameter expansion: ${#var}. To get the number of words, use set and the special parameter $#:

```
set -f
set -- $var
echo $#
```

To get the number of lines, use this:

```
IFS=$'\n'
set -f
set -- $var
echo $#
```

Regular Expressions

Regular expressions (often called *regexes* or *regexps*) are a more powerful form of pattern matching than file name globbing and can express a much wider range of patterns more precisely. They range from very simple (a letter or number is a regex that matches itself) to the mind-bogglingly complex. Long expressions are built with a concatenation of shorter expressions and, when broken down, are hard to understand.

There are similarities between regexes and file-globbing patterns: a list of characters within square brackets matches any of the characters in the list. An asterisk matches zero or more—not any character as in file expansion—of the preceding character. A dot matches any character, so `.*` matches any string of any length, much as an asterisk does in a globbing pattern.

Three important commands use regular expressions: grep, sed, and awk. The first is used for searching files, the second for editing files, and the third for almost anything because it is a complete programming language in its own right.

grep

grep searches files on the command line, or the standard input if no files are given, and prints lines matching a string or regular expression.

```
$ grep ':0[57]0:001:' "$kjv" | cut -c -78
Genesis:050:001:And Joseph fell upon his father's face, and wept upon him, and
Psalms:050:001:The mighty God, even the LORD, hath spoken, and called the eart
Psalms:070:001:MAKE HASTE, O GOD, TO DELIVER ME; MAKE HASTE TO HELP ME, O LORD
Isaiah:050:001:Thus saith the LORD, Where is the bill of your mother's divorce
Jeremiah:050:001:The word that the LORD spake against Babylon and against the
```

The shell itself could have done the job:

```
while read line
do
  case $line in
    *0[57]0:001:*) printf "%s\n" "${line:0:78}" ;;
  esac
done < "$kjv"
```

but it takes many times longer.

Often grep and other external commands are used to select a small number of lines from a file and pipe the results to a shell script for further processing:

```
$ grep 'Psalms:023' "$kjv" |
> {
> total=0
> while IFS=: read book chapter verse text
> do
>   set -- $text  ## put the verse into the positional parameters
>   total=$(( $total + $# )) ## add the number of parameters
> done
> echo $total
> }
118
```

grep should *not* be used to check whether one string is contained in another. For that, there is case or bash's expression evaluator, [[...]].

sed

For replacing a string or pattern with another string, nothing beats the stream editor sed. It is also good for pulling a particular line or range of lines from a file. To get the first three lines of the book of Leviticus and convert the name of the book to uppercase, you'd use this:

```
$ sed -n '/Lev.*:001:001/,/Lev.*:001:003/ s/Leviticus/LEVITICUS/p' "$kjv" |
> cut -c -78
LEVITICUS:001:001:And the LORD called unto Moses, and spake unto him out of th
LEVITICUS:001:002:Speak unto the children of Israel, and say unto them, If any
LEVITICUS:001:003:If his offering be a burnt sacrifice of the herd, let him of
```

The -n option tells sed not to print anything unless specifically told to do so; the default is to print all lines whether modified or not. The two regexes, enclosed in slashes and separated by a comma, define a range from the line that matches the first one to the line that matches the second; s is a command to search and replace and is probably the most often used.

When modifying a file, the standard Unix practice is to save the output to a new file and then move it to the place of the old one if the command is successful:

```
sed 's/this/that/g' "$file" > tempfile && mv tempfile "$file"
```

Some recent versions of sed have an -i option that will change the file *in situ*. If used, the option should be given a suffix to make a backup copy in case the script mangles the original irretrievably:

```
sed -i.bak 's/this/that/g' "$file"
```

More complicated scripts are possible with sed, but they quickly become very hard to read. This example is far from the worst I've seen, but it takes much more than a glance to figure out what it is doing. (It searches for *Jesus wept* and prints lines containing it along with the lines before and after; you can find a commented version at http://www.grymoire.com/Unix/Sed.html.)

```
sed -n '
/Jesus wept/ !{
    h
}
/Jesus wept/ {
    N
    x
    G
    p
    a\
---
    s/.*\n.*\n\(.*\)$/\1/
    h
}' "$kjv"
```

As you'll see shortly, the same program in awk is comparatively easy to understand.

There will be more examples of sed in later chapters, so we'll move on with the usual admonishment that external commands should be used on files, not strings. '*Nuff sed!*

awk

awk is a pattern scanning and processing language. An awk script is composed of one or more condition-action pairs. The condition is applied to each line in the file or files passed on the command line or to the standard input if no files are given. When the condition resolves successfully, the corresponding action is performed.

The condition may be a regular expression, a test of a variable, an arithmetic expression, or anything that produces a nonzero or nonempty result. It may represent a range by giving two condition separated by a comma; once a line matches the first condition, the action is performed until a line matches the second condition. For example, this condition matches input lines 10 to 20 inclusive (NR is a variable that contains the current line number):

```
NR == 10, NR == 20
```

There are two special conditions, BEGIN and END. The action associated with BEGIN is performed before any lines are read. The END action is performed after all the lines have been read or another action executes an exit statement.

The action can be any computation task. It can modify the input line, it can save it in a variable, it can perform a calculation on it, it can print some or all of the line, and it can do anything else you can think of.

Either the condition or the action may be missing. If there is no condition, the action is applied to all lines. If there is no action, matching lines are printed.

Each line is split into fields based on the contents of the variable FS. By default, it is any whitespace. The fields are numbered: $1, $2, and so on. $0 contains the entire line. The variable NF contains the number of fields in the line.

In the awk version of the kjvfirsts script, the field separator is changed to a colon using the -F command-line option (Listing 8-2). There is no condition, so the action is performed for every line. It splits the fourth field, the verse itself, into words, and then it prints the first three fields and the first word of the verse.

Listing 8-2. kjvfirsts-awk, Print Book, Chapter, Verse, and First Words from the KJV

```
awk -F: '  ## -F: sets the field delimiter to a colon
{
 ## split the fourth field into an array of words
 split($4,words," ")
 ## printf the first three fields and the first word of the fourth
 printf "%s %s:%s %s\n", $1, $2, $3, words[1]
}' "$kjv"
```

To find the shortest verse in the KJV, the next script checks the length of the fourth field. If it is less than the value of the shortest field seen so far, its length (minus the length of the name of the book), measured with the length() function, is stored in min, and the line is stored in verse. At the end, the line stored in verse is printed.

```
$ awk -F: 'BEGIN { min = 999 } ## set min larger than any verse length
length($0) - length($1) < min {
   min = length($0) - length($1)
   verse = $0
 }
```

```
END { print verse }' "$kjv"
John:011:035:Jesus wept.
```

As promised, here is an awk script that searches for a string (in this case, *Jesus wept*) and prints it along with the previous and next lines:

```
awk '/Jesus wept/ {
    print previousline
    print $0
    n = 1
    next
    }
n == 1 {
    print $0
    print "---"
    n = 2
    }
    {
    previousline = $0
    }' "$kjv"
```

To total a column of numbers:

```
$ printf "%s\n" {12..34} | awk '{ total += $1 }
> END { print total }'
529
```

This has been a very rudimentary look at awk. There will be a few more awk scripts later in the book, but for a full understanding, there are various books on awk

- *The AWK Programming Language* by the language's inventors (Alfred V. Aho, Peter J. Weinberger, and Brian W. Kernighan)

- *sed & awk* by Dale Dougherty and Arnold Robbins

- *Effective awk Programming* by Arnold Robbins

Or start with the man page.

File Name Expansion Options

To show you the effects of the various file name expansion options, I'll use the sa command defined in Chapter 4 as well as pr4, a function that prints its arguments in four columns across the screen. I have sa implemented as a function that, along with pr4, I put in my .bashrc file:

```
sa()
{
    pre=: post=:
    printf "$pre%s$post\n" "$@"
}
```

The pr4 function prints its argument in four equal columns, truncating any string that is too long for its allotted space:

```
pr4()
{
    ## calculate column width
    local width=$(( (${COLUMNS:-80} - 2) / 4 ))

    ## Note that braces are necessary on the second $width to separate it from 's'
    local s=%-$width.${width}s
    printf "$s $s $s $s\n" "$@"
}
```

There are six shell options that affect the way in which file names are expanded. They are enabled and disabled with the shopt command using options -s and -u, respectively:

```
shopt -s extglob       ## enable the extglob option
shopt -u nocaseglob    ## disable the nocaseglob option
```

To demonstrate the various globbing options, we'll create a directory, cd to it, and put some empty files in it:

```
$ mkdir "$HOME/globfest" && cd "$HOME/globfest" || echo Failed >&2
$ touch {a..f}{0..9}{t..z}$RANDOM .{a..f}{0..9}$RANDOM
```

This has created 420 files beginning with a letter and 60 beginning with a dot. There are, for example, seven files beginning with a1:

```
$ sa a1*
:a1t18345:
:a1u18557:
:a1v12490:
:a1w22008:
:a1x6088:
:a1y28651:
:a1z18318:
```

nullglob

Normally, when a wildcard pattern doesn't match any files, the pattern remains the same:

```
$ sa *xy
:*xy:
```

If the nullglob option is set and there is no match, an empty string is returned:

```
$ shopt -s nullglob
$ sa *xy
::
$ shopt -u nullglob    ## restore the default behavior
```

failglob

If the `failglob` option is set and no files match a wildcard pattern, an error message is printed:

```
$ shopt -s failglob
$ sa *xy
bash: no match: *xy
$ shopt -u failglob    ## restore the default behavior
```

dotglob

A wildcard at the beginning of a file name expansion pattern does not match file names that begin with a dot. These are intended to be "hidden" files and are not matched by standard file name expansion:

```
$ sa * | wc -l  ## not dot files
420
```

To match "dot" files, the leading dot must be given explicitly:

```
$ sa .* | wc -l ## dot files; includes . and ..
62
```

The touch command at the beginning of this section created 60 dot files. The .* expansion shows 62 because it includes the hard-linked entries . and .. that are created in all subdirectories.

The `dotglob` option causes dot files to be matched just like any other files:

```
$ shopt -s dotglob
$ printf "%s\n" * | wc -l
480
```

Expansions of *, with dotglob enabled, do not include the hard links . and ...

extglob

When extended globbing is turned on with `shopt -s extglob`, five new file name expansion operators are added. In each case, the `pattern-list` is a list of pipe-separated globbing patterns. It is enclosed in parentheses, which are preceded by ?, *, +, @, or !, for example, +(a[0-2]|34|2u), ?(john|paul|george|ringo).

To demonstrate extended globbing, remove the existing files in $HOME/globfest, and create a new set:

```
$ cd $HOME/globfest
$ rm *
$ touch {john,paul,george,ringo}{john,paul,george,ringo}{1,2}$RANDOM\
> {john,paul,george,ringo}{1,2}$RANDOM{,,} {1,2}$RANDOM{,,,}
```

?(pattern-list)

This `pattern-list` matches zero or one occurrence of the given patterns. For example, the pattern `?(john|paul)2` matches john2, paul2, and 2:

```
$ pr4 ?(john|paul)2*
222844              228151              231909              232112
john214726          john216085          john26              paul218047
paul220720          paul231051
```

*(pattern-list)

This is like the previous form, but it matches zero or more occurrences of the given patterns; `*(john|paul)2` will match all files matched in the previous example, as well as those that have either pattern more than once in succession:

```
pr4 *(john|paul)2*
222844              228151              231909              232112
john214726          john216085          john26              johnjohn23185
johnpaul25000       paul218047          paul220720          paul231051
pauljohn221365      paulpaul220101
```

@(pattern-list)

The pattern `@(john|paul)2` matches files that have a single instance of either pattern followed by a 2:

```
$ pr4 @(john|paul)2*
john214726          john216085          john26              paul218047
paul220720          paul231051
```

+(pattern-list)

The pattern `+(john|paul)2` matches files that begin with one or more instances of a pattern in the list followed by a 2:

```
$ pr4 +(john|paul)2*
john214726          john216085          john26              johnjohn23185
johnpaul25000       paul218047          paul220720          paul231051
pauljohn221365      paulpaul220101
```

!(pattern-list)

The last extended globbing pattern matches anything except one of the given patterns. It differs from the rest in that each pattern must match the entire file name. The pattern `!(r|p|j)*` will not exclude files beginning with r, p, or j (or any others), but the following pattern will (and will also exclude files beginning with a number):

```
$ pr4 !([jpr0-9]*)
george115425          george132443          george1706           george212389
george223300          george27803           georgegeorge16122    georgegeorge28573
georgejohn118699      georgejohn29502       georgepaul12721      georgepaul222618
georgeringo115095     georgeringo227768
```

■ **Note** The explanation given here for the last of these patterns is simplified but should be enough to cover its use in the vast majority of cases. For a more complete explanation, see Chapter 9 in *From Bash to Z Shell* (Apress, 2005).

---

nocaseglob

When the nocaseglob option is set, lowercase letters match uppercase letters, and vice versa:

```
$ cd $HOME/globfest
$ rm -rf *
$ touch {{a..d},{A..D}}$RANDOM
$ pr4 *
A31783                B31846                C17836               D14046
a31882                b31603                c29437               d26729
```

The default behavior is for a letter to match only those of the same case:

```
$ pr4 [ab]*
a31882                b31603
```

The nocaseglob option causes a letter to match both cases:

```
$ shopt -s nocaseglob
$ pr4 [ab]*
A31783                B31846                a31882               b31603
```

globstar

Introduced in bash-4.0, the globstar option allows the use of ** to descend recursively into directories and subdirectories looking for matching files. As an example, create a hierarchy of directories:

```
$ cd $HOME/globfest
$ rm -rf *
$ mkdir -p {ab,ac}$RANDOM/${RANDOM}{q1,q2}/{z,x}$(( $RANDOM % 10 ))
```

The double asterisk wildcard expands to all the directories:

```
$ shopt -s globstar
$ pr4 **
```

```
ab11278          ab11278/22190q1      ab11278/22190q1/z7    ab1394
ab1394/10985q2   ab1394/10985q2/x5    ab4351                ab4351/23041q1
ab4351/23041q1/x1 ab4424              ab4424/8752q2         ab4424/8752q2/z9
ac11393          ac11393/20940q1      ac11393/20940q1/z4    ac17926
ac17926/19435q2  ac17926/19435q2/x0   ac23443               ac23443/5703q2
ac23443/5703q2/z4 ac5662              ac5662/17958q1        ac5662/17958q1/x4
```

Summary

Many external commands deal with files. In this chapter, I have covered the most important ones and those that are most often misused. They have not been covered in detail, and some emphasis has been placed on how to avoid calling them when the shell can do the same job more efficiently. Basically, it boils down to this: *use external commands to process files, not strings.*

Shell Options

- nullglob: Returns null string if no files match pattern

- failglob: Prints error message if no files match

- dotglob: Includes dot files in pattern matching

- extglob: Enables extended file name expansion patterns

- nocaseglob: Matches files ignoring case differences

- globstar: Searches file hierarchy for matching files

External Commands

- awk: Is a pattern scanning and processing language

- cat: Concatenates files and print on the standard output

- cut: Removes sections from each line of one or more files

- grep: Prints lines matching a pattern

- head: Outputs the first part of one or more files

- ls: Lists directory contents

- sed: Is a stream editor for filtering and transforming text

- touch: Changes file timestamps

- wc: Counts lines, words, and characters in one or more files

Exercises

1. Modify the kjvfirsts script accept a command-line argument that specifies how many chapters are to be printed.

2. Why are the chapter and verse numbers in kjvfirsts formatted with %s instead of %d?

3. Write an awk script to find the longest verse in KJV.

■ ■ ■

## CHAPTER 9

Reserved Words and Builtin Commands

There are almost 60 builtin commands and more than 20 reserved words in bash. Some of them are indispensable, and some are rarely used in scripts. Some are used primarily at the command line, and some are seldom seen anywhere. Some have been discussed already, and others will be used extensively in future chapters.

The reserved words (also called *keywords*) are !, case, coproc, do, done, elif, else, esac, fi, for, function, if, in, select, then, until, while, {, }, time, [[, and]]. All except coproc, select, and time have been covered earlier in the book.

In addition to the standard commands, new builtin commands can be dynamically loaded into the shell at runtime. The bash source code package has more than 20 such commands ready to be compiled.

Because keywords and builtin commands are part of the shell itself, they execute much faster than external commands. They do not have to start a new process, and they have access to, and can change, the shell's environment.

This chapter looks at some of the more useful reserved words and builtin commands, examining some in detail and some with a summary; a few are deprecated. Many more are described elsewhere in the book. For the rest, there is the builtins man page and the help builtin.

help, Display Information About Builtin Commands

The help command prints brief information about the usage of builtin commands and reserved words. With the -s option, it prints a usage synopsis.

Two new options are available with bash-4.0: -d and -m. The first prints a short, one-line description of the command; the latter formats the output in the style of a man page:

```
$ help -m help
NAME
    help - Display information about builtin commands.

SYNOPSIS
    help [-dms] [pattern ...]

DESCRIPTION
    Display information about builtin commands.

    Displays brief summaries of builtin commands.  If PATTERN is
    specified, gives detailed help on all commands matching PATTERN,
    otherwise the list of help topics is printed.
```

```
Options:
  -d        output short description for each topic
  -m        display usage in pseudo-manpage format
  -s        output only a short usage synopsis for each topic matching
     PATTERN

Arguments:
  PATTERN   Pattern specifying a help topic

Exit Status:
Returns success unless PATTERN is not found or an invalid option is given.
```

```
SEE ALSO
    bash(1)

IMPLEMENTATION
    GNU bash, version 4.0.24(1)-release (i686-pc-linux-gnuoldld)
    Copyright (C) 2009 Free Software Foundation, Inc.
    License GPLv3+: GNU GPL version 3 or later <http://gnu.org/licenses/gpl.html>
```

The pattern is a globbing pattern, in which * matches any number of any characters and [...] matches any single character in the enclosed list. Without any wildcard, a trailing * is assumed:

```
$ help -d '*le' tr ## show commands ending in le and beginning with tr
Shell commands matching keyword `*le, tr'

enable - Enable and disable shell builtins.
mapfile - Read lines from the standard input into an array variable.
while - Execute commands as long as a test succeeds.
trap - Trap signals and other events.
true - Return a successful result.
```

time, Print Time Taken for Execution of a Command

The reserved word, time, prints the time it takes for a command to execute. The command can be a simple or compound command or a pipeline. The default output appears on three lines, showing the real time, user CPU time, and system CPU time that was taken by the command:

```
$ time echo {1..30000} >/dev/null 2>&1


real    0m0.175s
user    0m0.152s
sys     0m0.017s
```

You can modify this output by changing the TIMEFORMAT variable:

```
$ TIMEFORMAT='%R seconds  %P%% CPU usage'
$ time echo {1..30000} >/dev/null
0.153 seconds  97.96% CPU usage
```

The appendix contains a full description of the TIMEFORMAT variable.

A frequently asked question about the time command is, "Why can't I redirect the output of time?" The answer demonstrates a difference between a reserved word and a builtin command. When the shell executes a command, the process is strictly defined (see Chapter 4). A shell keyword doesn't have to follow that procedure. In the case of time, the entire command line (with the exception of the keyword itself but including the redirection) is passed to the shell to execute. When the command has completed, the timing information is printed.

To redirect the output of time, enclose it in braces:

```
$ { time echo {1..30000} >/dev/null 2>&1 ; } 2> numlisttime
$ cat numlisttime
0.193 seconds  90.95% CPU usage
```

read, Read a Line from an Input Stream

If read has no arguments, bash reads a line from its standard input stream and stores it in the variable REPLY. If the input contains a backslash at the end of a line, it and the following newline are removed, and the next line is read, joining the two lines:

```
$ printf "%s\n" '   First line   \' '   Second line   ' | {
> read
> sa "$REPLY"
> }
:   First line       Second line   :
```

■ **Note** The braces ({ }) in this and the following snippets create a common subshell for both the read and sa commands. Without them, read would be in a subshell by itself, and sa would not see the new value of REPLY (or of any other variable set in the subshell).

Only one option, -r, is part of the POSIX standard. The many bash options (-a, -d, -e, -n, -p, -s, -n, -t, -u, and, new to bash-4.0, -i) are part of what makes this shell work so well for interactive scripts.

-r, Read Backslashes Literally

With the -r option, backslashes are treated literally:

```
$ printf "%s\n" '   First line\' "   Second line   " | {
> read -r
> read line2
> sa "$REPLY" "$line2"
> }
:   First line\:
:Second line:
```

The second read in that snippet supplies a variable to store the input rather than using REPLY. As a result, it applies word splitting to the input, and leading and trailing spaces are removed. If IFS had been set to an empty string, then spaces would not be used for word splitting:

```
$ printf "%s\n" '   First line\' "   Second line    " | {
> read -r
> IFS= read line2
> sa "$REPLY" "$line2"
> }
:    First line\:
:    Second line    :
```

If more than one variable is given on the command line, the first field is stored in the first variable, and subsequent fields are stored in the following variables. If there are more fields than variables, the last one stores the remainder of the line:

```
$ printf "%s\n" "first second third fourth fifth sixth" | {
> read a b c d
> sa "$a" "$b" "$c" "$d"
> }
:first:
:second:
:third:
:fourth fifth sixth:
```

-e, Get Input with the readline Library

When at the command line or when using read with the -e option to get input from the keyboard, the readline library is used. It allows full line editing. The default editing style, found in most shells, only allows editing by erasing the character to the left of the cursor with a backspace.

With -e, a backspace still works, of course, but the cursor can be moved over the entire line character by character with the arrow keys or with Ctrl-B and Ctrl-N for backward and forward, respectively. Ctrl-A moves to the beginning of the line, and Ctrl-E moves to the end.

In addition, other readline commands can be bound to whatever key combinations you like. I have Ctrl-left arrow bound to backward-word and Ctrl-right arrow to forward-word. Such bindings can be placed in $HOME/.inputrc. Mine has entries for two terminals, rxvt and xterm:

```
"\e0d": backward-word      ## rxvt
"\e0c": forward-word       ## rxvt
"\e[1;5D": backward-word   ## xterm
"\e[1;5C": forward-word    ## xterm
```

To check the code to use in your terminal emulation, press ^V (Ctrl-v) and then the key combination you want. For example, in xterm, I see ^[[1;5D when I press Ctrl-left arrow.

-a, Read Words into an Array

The -a option assigns the words read to an array, starting at index zero:

```
$ printf "%s\n" "first second third fourth fifth sixth" | {
> read -a array
> sa "${array[0]}"
> sa "${array[5]}"
> }
:first:
:sixth:
```

-d DELIM, Read Until DELIM Instead of a Newline

The -d option takes an argument that changes read's delimiter from a newline to the first character of that argument:

```
$ printf "%s\n" "first second third fourth fifth sixth" | {
> read -d ' nrh' a
> read -d 'nrh' b
> read -d 'rh' c
> read -d 'h' d
> sa "$a" "$b" "$c" "$d"
> }
:first:          ## -d ' '
:seco:           ## -d n
:d thi:          ## -d r
:d fourt:        ## -d h
```

-n NUM, Read a Maximum of NUM Characters

Most frequently used when a single character (for example, y or n) is required, read returns after reading NUM characters rather than waiting for a newline. It is often used in conjunction with -s.

-s, Do Not Echo Input Coming from a Terminal

Useful for entering passwords and single-letter responses, the -s option suppresses the display of the keystrokes entered.

-p PROMPT:, Output PROMPT Without a Trailing Newline

The following snippet is a typical use of these three options:

```
read -sn1 -p "Continue (y/n)? " var
case ${var^} in  ## bash 4.0, convert $var to uppercase
  Y) ;;
  N) printf "\n%s\n" "Good bye."
     exit
     ;;
esac
```

When run, it looks like this when n or N is entered:

```
Continue (y/n)?
Good bye.
```

-t TIMEOUT, Only Wait TIMEOUT Seconds for Complete Input

The -t option was introduced in bash-2.04 and accepts integers greater than 0 as an argument. If TIMEOUT seconds pass before a complete line has been entered, read exits with failure; any characters already entered are left in the input stream for the next command that reads the standard input.

In bash-4.0, the -t option accepts a value of 0 and returns successfully if there is input waiting to be read. It also accepts fractional arguments in decimal format:

```
read -t .1 var  ## timeout after one-tenth of a second
read -t 2 var   ## timeout after 2 seconds
```

Setting the variable TMOUT to an integer greater than zero has the same effect as the -t option. In bash-4.0, a decimal fraction can also be used.

```
$ TMOUT=2.5
$ TIMEFORMAT='%R seconds   %P%% CPU usage'
$ time read
2.500 seconds   0.00% CPU usage
```

-u FD: Read from File Descriptor FD Instead of the Standard Input

The -u option tells bash to read from a file descriptor. Given this file:

```
First line
Second line
Third line
Fourth line
```

this script reads from it, alternating between redirection and the -u option, and prints all four lines:

```
exec 3<$HOME/txt
read var <&3
echo "$var"
read -u3 var
echo "$var"
read var <&3
echo "$var"
read -u3 var
echo "$var"
```

-i TEXT, Use TEXT as the Initial Text for readline

New to bash-4.0, the -i option, used in conjunction with the -e option, places text on the command line for editing.

```
$ read -ei 'Edit this' -p '==> '
==> Edit this
```

The bash-4.0 script shown in Listing 9-1 loops, showing a spinning busy indicator, until the user presses a key. It uses four read options: -s, -n, -p, and -t.

Listing 9-1. spinner, Show Busy Indicator While Waiting for User to Press a Key

```
spinner="\|/-"              ## spinner
chars=1                     ## number of characters to display
delay=.15                   ## time in seconds between characters
prompt="press any key..."   ## user prompt
clearline="\e[K"            ## clear to end of line (ANSI terminal)
CR="\r"                     ## carriage return

## loop until user presses a key
until read -sn1 -t$delay -p "$prompt" var
do
  printf "  %.${chars}s$CR" "$spinner"
  temp=${spinner#?}                  ## remove first character from $spinner
  spinner=$temp${spinner%"$temp"} ## and add it to the end
done
printf "$CR$clearline"
```

If delay is changed to an integer, the script will work in all versions of bash, but the spinner will be very slow.

eval, Expand Arguments and Execute Resulting Command

In Chapter 5, the eval builtin was used to get the value of a variable whose name was in another variable. It accomplished the same task as bash's variable expansion, ${!var}. What actually happened was that eval expanded the variable inside quotation marks; the backslashes removed the special meanings of the quotes and the dollar sign so that they remained the literal characters. The resulting string was then executed:

```
$ x=yes
$ a=x
$ eval "sa \"\$$a\"" ## executes: sa "$x"
yes
```

Other uses of eval include assigning values to a variable whose name is contained in another variable and obtaining more than one value from a single command.

Poor Man's Arrays

Before bash had associative arrays (that is, before version 4.0), they could be simulated with eval. These two functions set and retrieve such values and take them for a test run (Listing 9-2).

Listing 9-2. varfuncs, Emulate Associative Arrays

```
validname() ## Borrowed from Chapter 7
 case $1 in
   [!a-zA-Z_]* | *[!a-zA-Z0-9_]* ) return 1;;
 esac

setvar() #@ DESCRIPTION: assign value to supplied name
{        #@ USAGE: setvar varname value
  validname "$1" || return 1
  eval "$1=\$2"
}

getvar() #@ DESCRIPTION: print value assigned to varname
{        #@ USAGE: getvar varname
  validname "$1" || return 1
  eval "printf '%s\n' \"\${$1}\""
}

echo "Assigning some values"
for n in {1..3}
do
  setvar "var_$n" "$n - $RANDOM"
done
echo "Variables assigned; printing values:"
for n in {1..3}
do
 getvar "var_$n"
done
```

Here's a sample run:

```
Assigning some values
Variables assigned; printing values:
1 - 28538
2 - 22523
3 - 19362
```

Note the assignment in setvar. Compare it with this:

```
setvar() { eval "$1=\"$2\""; }
```

If you substitute this function for the one in varfuncs and run the script, the results look very much the same. What's the difference? Let's try it with a different value, using stripped-down versions of the functions at the command line:

```
$ {
> setvar() { eval "$1=\$2"; }
> getvar() { eval "printf '%s\n' \"\${$1}\""; }
> n=1
> setvar "qwerty_$n" 'xxx " echo Hello"'
> getvar "qwerty_$n"
> }
xxx " echo hello"
$ {
> setvar2() { eval "$1=\"$2\""; }
> setvar2 "qwerty_$n" 'xxx " echo Hello"'
> }
Hello
```

Hello? Where did that come from? With set -x, you can see exactly what is happening:

```
$ set -x ## shell will now print commands and arguments as they are executed
$ setvar "qwerty_$n" 'xxx " echo Hello"'
+ setvar qwerty_1 'xxx " echo Hello"'
+ eval 'qwerty_1=$2'
```

The last line is the important one. There the variable qwerty_1 is set to whatever is in $2. $2 is not expanded or interpreted in any way; its value is simply assigned to qwerty_1.

```
$ setvar2 "qwerty_$n" 'xxx " echo Hello"'
+ setvar2 qwerty_1 'xxx " echo Hello"'
+ eval 'qwerty_1="xxx " echo Hello""'
++ qwerty_1='xxx '
++ echo HelloHello
```

In this version, $2 is expanded before the assignment and is therefore subject to word splitting; eval sees an assignment followed by a command. The assignment is made, and then the command is executed. In this case, the command was harmless, but if the value had been entered by a user, it could have been something dangerous.

To use eval safely, ensure that the unexpanded variable is presented for assignment using eval "$var=\$value". If necessary, combine multiple elements into one variable before using eval:

```
string1=something
string2='rm -rf *' ## we do NOT want this to be executed
eval "$var=\"Example=$string1\" $string2" ## WRONG!! Files gone!
combo="Example=$string1 $string2"
eval "$var=\$combo" ## RIGHT!
```

The value of the variable whose name is in var is now the same as the contents of combo, if var was set to xx:

```
$ printf "%s\n" "$xx"
Example=something rm -rf *
```

Setting Multiple Variables from One Command

I have seen many scripts in which several variables are set to components of the date and time using this (or something similar):

```
year=$(date +%Y)
month=$(date +%m)
day=$(date +%d)
hour=$(date +%H)
minute=$(date +%M)
second=$(date +%S)
```

This is inefficient because it calls the date command six times. It could also give the wrong results. What happens if the script is called a fraction of a second before midnight and the date changes between setting the month and day? The script was called at 2009-05-31T23:59:59 (this is the ISO standard format for date and time), but the values assigned could amount to 2009-05-01T00:00:00. The date that was wanted was 31 May 2009 23:59:59 or 01 June 2009 00:00:00; what the script got was 1 May 2009 00:00:00. That's a whole month off!

A better method is to get a single string from date and split it into its parts:

```
date=$(date +%Y-%m-%dT%H:%M:%S)
time=${date#*T}
date=${date%T*}
year=${date%%-*}
daymonth=${date#*-}
month=${daymonth%-*}
day=${daymonth#*-}
hour=${time%%:*}
minsec=${time#*-}
minute=${minsec%-*}
second=${minsec#*-}
```

Better still, use eval:

```
$ eval "$(date "+year=%Y month=%m day=%d hour=%H minute=%M second=%S")"
```

The output of the date command is executed by eval:

```
year=2009 month=05 day=31 hour=23 minute=59 second=59
```

The last two methods use only one call to date, so the variables are all populated using the same timestamp. They both take about the same amount of time, which is a fraction of the time of multiple calls to date. The clincher is that the eval method is about one third as long as the string-splitting method.

type, Display Information About Commands

Many people use which to find out the actual command that will be used when one is executed. There are two problems with that.

First is that there are at least two versions of which, one of which is a csh script that doesn't work well in a Bourne-type shell (thankfully, this version is becoming very rare). The second problem is that which is an external command, and it cannot know exactly what the shell will do with any given command. All it does is search the directories in the PATH variable for an executable with the same name.

```
$ which echo printf
/bin/echo
/usr/bin/printf
```

You know that both echo and printf are builtin commands, but which doesn't know that. Instead of which, use the shell builtin type:

```
$ type echo printf sa
echo is a shell builtin
printf is a shell builtin
sa is a function
sa ()
{
    pre=: post=:;
    printf "$pre%s$post\n" "$@"
}
```

When there's more than one possible command that would be executed for a given name, they can all be shown by using the -a option:

```
$ type -a echo printf
echo is a shell builtin
echo is /bin/echo
printf is a shell builtin
printf is /usr/bin/printf
```

The -p option limits the search to files and does not give any information about builtins, functions, or aliases. If the shell executes the command internally, nothing will be printed unless the -a option is also given:

```
$ type -p echo printf sa time  ## no outpus as no files would be executed
$ type -ap echo printf sa time
/bin/echo
/usr/bin/printf
/usr/chris/bin/sa
/usr/bin/time
```

Or you can use -P:

```
$ type -P echo printf sa time
/bin/echo
/usr/bin/printf
/usr/chris/bin/sa
/usr/bin/time
```

The -t option gives a single word for each command, either alias, keyword, function, builtin, file, or an empty string:

```
$ type -t echo printf sa time ls
builtin
builtin
function
keyword
file
```

The type command fails if any of its arguments are not found.

builtin, Execute a Builtin Command

The argument to builtin is a shell builtin command that will be called rather than a function with the same name. It prevents the function from calling itself and calling itself *ad nauseam*.

```
cd() #@ DESCRIPTION: change directory and display 10 most recent files
{     #@ USAGE: cd DIR
  builtin cd "$@" || return 1 ## don't call function recursively
  ls -t | head
}
```

command, Execute a Command or Display Information About Commands

With -v or -V, display information about a command. Without options, call the command from an external file rather than a function.

pwd, Print the Current Working Directory

pwd prints the absolute pathname of the current directory. With the -P option, it prints the physical location with no symbolic links.

```
$ ls -ld $HOME/Chess  ## Directory is a symbolic link
lrwxrwxrwx  1 chris chris 10 Feb 15  2008 /home/chris/Chess -> work/Chess
$ cd $HOME/Chess
$ pwd                 ## Include symbolic links
/home/chris/Chess
$ pwd -P              ## Print physical location with no links
/home/chris/work/Chess
```

unalias, Remove One or More Aliases

In my `~/.bashrc` file, I have `unalias -a` to remove all aliases. Some GNU/Linux distributions make the dangerous mistake of defining aliases that replace standard commands.

One of the worst examples is the redefinition of `rm` (remove files or directories) to `rm -i`. If a person, used to being prompted before a file is removed, puts `rm *` (for example) in a script, all the files will be gone without any prompting. Aliases are not exported and, by default, not run in shell scripts even if defined.

Deprecated Builtins

I don't recommend using the following deprecated builtin commands:

- `alias`: Defines an alias. As the `bash` man page says, "For almost every purpose, aliases are superseded by shell functions."

- `let`: Evaluates arithmetic expressions. Use the POSIX syntax `$(( expression ))` instead.

- `select`: Is an inflexible menuing command. Much better menus can be written easily with the shell.

- `typeset`: Declares a variable's attributes and, in a function, restricts a variable's scope to that function and its children. Use `local` to restrict a variable's scope to a function, and use `declare` to set any other attributes (if necessary).

Dynamically Loadable Builtins

Bash can load new builtin commands at runtime if and when needed. The bash source package has a directory full of examples ready to be compiled. To do that, download the source from `ftp://ftp.cwru.edu/pub/bash/`. Unpack the tarball, `cd` into the top level directory, and run the configure script:

```
version=4.0 ## or use your bash version (but I recommend 4.0)
wget ftp://ftp.cwru.edu/pub/bash/bash-$version.tar.gz
gunzip bash-$version.tar.gz
tar xf bash-$version.tar
cd bash-$version
./configure
```

The `configure` script creates makefiles throughout the source tree, including one in `examples/loadables`. In that directory are the source files for builtin versions of a number of standard commands, as the `README` file says, "whose execution time is dominated by process startup time." You can `cd` into that directory and run `make`:

```
cd examples/loadables
make
```

You'll now have a number of commands ready to load into your shell. These include the following:

```
logname   tee      head     mkdir    rmdir     uname
ln        cat      id       whoami
```

There are also some useful new commands:

```
print      ## Compatible with the ksh print command
finfo      ## Print file information
strftime   ## Format date and time
```

These builtins can be loaded into a running shell with the following:

```
enable -f filename built-in-name
```

The files include documentation, and the `help` command can be used with them, just as with other builtin commands:

```
$ enable -f ./strftime strftime
$ help strftime
strftime: strftime format [seconds]
    Converts date and time format to a string and displays it on the
    standard output.  If the optional second argument is supplied, it
    is used as the number of seconds since the epoch to use in the
    conversion, otherwise the current time is used.
```

For information on writing dynamically loadable builtin commands, see my article at http://cfaj.freeshell.org/shell/articles/dynamically-loadable/.

Summary

You learned about the following commands in this chapter.

Commands and Reserved Words

- `builtin`: Executes a builtin command

- `command`: Executes an external command or print information about a command

- `eval`: Executes arguments as a shell command.

- `help`: Displays information about builtin commands.

- `pwd`: Prints the current working directory

- `read`: Reads a line from the standard input and splits it into fields

- `time`: Reports time consumed by pipeline's execution

- `type`: Displays information about command type

Deprecated Commands

- `alias`: Defines or display aliases

- `let`: Evaluates arithmetic expressions

- `select`: Selects words from a list and execute commands

- `typeset`: Sets variable values and attributes

Exercises

1. Write a script that stores the time it takes a command (your choice of command) to run in three variables, `real`, `user`, and `system`, corresponding to the three default times that `time` prints.

## CHAPTER 10

Writing Bug-Free Scripts and Debugging the Rest

The programmer who has never written a buggy program is a figment of someone's imagination. Bugs are the bane of a programmer's existence. They range from simple typing errors to bad coding to faulty logic. Some are easily fixed; others can take hours of hunting.

At one end of the spectrum are the syntax errors that prevent a script from completing or running at all. These may involve a missing character: a space, a bracket or brace, a quotation mark. It may be a mistyped command or variable name. It may be a missing keyword, such as then after elif.

At the other end of the spectrum are the errors in logic. It may be counting from 1 when you should have started at 0, or it may be using -gt (greater than) when it should have been -ge (greater than or equal to). It may be a faulty formula (isn't Fahrenheit to Celsius (F - 32) * 1.8?) or using the wrong field in a data record (I thought the shell was field 5 in /etc/passwd!).

In between the extremes, common errors include trying to operate on the wrong type of data (either the program itself supplied the wrong data or an external source did) and failing to check that a command succeeds before proceeding to the next step.

This chapter looks at various techniques to get a program doing what it is supposed to, including the various shell options for checking and following a script's progress, strategically placing debugging instructions, and, most important, preventing bugs in the first place.

Prevention Is Better Than Cure

It is far better to avoid introducing bugs than to remove them. There's no way to guarantee bug-free scripts, but a number of precautions can reduce the frequency considerably. Making your code easy to read helps. So does documenting it, so that you know what it's for, what it expects, what results it produces, and so on.

Structure Your Programs

The term *structured programming* is applied to various programming paradigms, but they all involve modular programming—breaking the problem down into manageable parts. In developing a large application with the shell, this means either functions, separate scripts, or a combination of both.

Even a short program can benefit from some structure; it should contain discrete sections:

- Comments
- Initialization of variables
- Function definitions

- Runtime configuration (parse options, read configuration file, and so on)

- Sanity check (are all values reasonable?)

- Process information (calculate, slice and dice lines, I/O, and so on)

Using this outline, all the components of a short but complete script are presented in the following sections. There are errors in the script; these will be found and corrected using various debugging techniques.

Comments

The comments should include metadata about the script, including a description, a synopsis of how to call the command or function, author, date of creation, date of last revision, version number, options, and any other information that is needed in order to run the command successfully.

```
#:      Title: wfe - List words ending with PATTERN
#:   Synopsis: wfe [-c|-h|-v] REGEX
#:       Date: 2009-04-13
#:    Version: 1.0
#:     Author: Chris F.A. Johnson
#:    Options: -c - Include compound words
#:             -h - Print usage information
#:             -v - Print version number
```

I have used #: to introduce these comments so that grep '^#:' wfe will extract all the metadata.

Initialization of Variables

First define some variables containing metadata. There will be some duplication with the previous comments, but these variables may be needed later:

```
## Script metadata
scriptname=${0##*/}
description="List words ending with REGEX"
usage="$scriptname [-c|-h|-v] REGEX"
date_of_creation=2009-04-13
version=1.0
author="Chris F.A. Johnson"
```

Then define the default values, file locations, and other information needed by this script:

```
## File locations
dict=$HOME
wordfile=$dict/singlewords
conpoundfile=$dict/Compounds

## Default is not to show compound words
compounds=

## Regular expression supplied on the command line
pattern=$1
```

Function Definitions

There are three functions that I include in my scripts (apart from quick-and-dirty one-offs). They are die, usage, and version; they may be included in the script itself or in a function library sourced by the script. I haven't usually included them in the scripts in this book; that would be unnecessarily repetitive.

```
## Function definitions
die() #@ DESCRIPTION: print error message and exit with supplied return code
{      #@ USAGE: die STATUS [MESSAGE]
  error=$1
  shift
  [ -n "$*" ] printf "%s\n" "$*" >&2
  exit "$error"
}

usage() #@ DESCRIPTION: print usage information
{        #@ USAGE: usage
         #@ REQUIRES: variable defined: $scriptname
  printf "%s - %s\n" "$scriptname" "$description"
  printf "USAGE: %s\n" "$usage"
}

version() #@ DESCRIPTION: print version information
{          #@ USAGE: version
           #@ REQUIRES: variables defined: $scriptname, $author and $version
  printf "%s version %s\n" "$scriptname" "$version"
  printf "by %s, %d\n" "$author"  "${date_of_creation%%-*"
}
```

Any other functions will follow right after these generic functions.

Runtime Configuration and Options

In Chapter 12, there is an in-depth look at runtime configuration and the different methods that can be used. Much of the time, all you need to do is parse the command-line options:

```
## parse command-line options, -c, -h, and -v
while getopts chv var
do
  case $var in
    c) compounds=$compoundfile ;;
    h) usage; exit ;;
    v) version; exit ;;
  esac
done
shift $(( $OPTIND - 1 ))
```

Process Information

As is often the case in a short script, the actual work of the script is relatively short; setting up parameters and checking the validity of data take up the greater part of the program.

```
## Search $wordfile and $compounds if it is defined
{
  cat "$wordfile"
  if [ -n "$compounds" ]
  then
    cut -f1 "$compounds"
  fi
} | grep -i ".$regex$" |
 sort -fu ## Case-insensitive sort; remove duplicates
```

Here, cat is necessary because the second file, whose location is stored in the compounds variable, cannot be given as an argument to grep because it is more than a list of words. The file has three tab-separated fields: the phrase with spaces and other nonalpha characters removed and the following letter capitalized, the original phrase, and the lengths as they would appear in a cryptic crossword puzzle:

```
corkScrew         cork-screw      (4-5)
groundCrew        ground crew     (6,4)
haveAScrewLoose have a screw loose      (4,1,5,5)
```

If it were a simple word list, like singlewords, the pipeline could have been replaced by a simple command:

```
grep -i ".$regex$" "$wordfile" ${compounds:+"$compounds"}
```

The grep command searches the files given on the command line for lines that match a regular expression. The -i option tells grep to consider uppercase and lowercase letters as equivalent.

Document Your Code

Until fairly recently, my own documentation habits left a lot to be desired. In my scripts directory, I have more than 900 programs written over the last 15 years or thereabouts. There are more than 90 function libraries. About 20 scripts are called by cron, and a dozen more are called by those scripts. There are probably about 100 scripts that I use regularly, with "regularly" being anything from several times a day to once or twice a year.

The rest are scripts under development, abandoned scripts, scripts that didn't work out, and scripts that I have no idea what they are for. I don't know what they are for because I didn't include any documentation, not even a one-line description. I don't know whether they work, whether I decided I didn't really need that script, or anything about them.

Many of them, I can tell what they do from the name. In others, the code is straightforward, and the purpose is obvious. But there are still many scripts whose purpose I don't know. Some of them I will probably end up duplicating when I need that task again. When I do, they'll have at least minimal documentation.

Format Your Code Consistently

There are various models for pretty printing code, and some people are quite vociferous in their defense of a particular style. I have my own preference (which you'll have noticed from the scripts in this book), but consistency is more important than the indentations being two, four, or six spaces per level. That there is indentation is more important than the amount of it. I would say that two spaces (which is what I use) is the minimum and that eight is the outside limit, if not too much.

Similarly, it doesn't matter whether you have then on the same line as if or not. Either of these is fine:

```
if [ "$var" = "yes" ]; then
  echo "Proceeding"
fi

if [ "$var" = "yes" ]
then
  echo "Proceeding"
fi
```

The same goes for other loops and function definitions. I prefer this:

```
funcname()
{
  : body here
}
```

Others like this:

```
funcname() {
  : body here
}
```

So long as the formatting is consistent and makes the structure clear, it doesn't matter which format you use.

The K.I.S.S. Principle

Simplicity aids in understanding the intent of your program, but it's not just keeping code as short as possible. When someone posted this question, my first thought was, "That will be a complicated regex." My second was that I wouldn't use a regular expression.

> *I need a regular expression to express financial quantities in American notation. They have a leading dollar sign and an optional string of asterisks, a string of decimal digits, and a fractional part consisting of a decimal point (.) and two decimal digits. The string to the left of the decimal point could be a single zero. Otherwise, it must not start with a zero. If there are more than three digits to the left of the decimal point, groups of three must be separated by commas. Example: $**2,345.67.*

I'd break the task down into discrete steps and code each one separately. For example, the first check I'd do would be this:

```
amount='$**2,345.67'
case $amount in
  \$[*0-9]*) ;; ## OK (dollar sign followed by asterisks or digits), do nothing
  *) exit 1 ;;
esac
```

By the time the tests are finished, there will be a lot more code than there would be in a regular expression, but it will be easier to understand and to change if the requirements change.

Grouping Commands

Rather than redirect each of several lines, group them with braces and use a single redirection. I saw this in a forum recently:

```
echo "user odad odd" > ftp.txt
echo "prompt" >> ftp.txt
echo "cd $i" >> ftp.txt
echo "ls -ltr" >> ftp.txt
echo "bye" >> ftp.txt
```

I recommended this instead:

```
{
  echo "user odad odd"
  echo "prompt"
  echo "cd $i"
  echo "ls -ltr"
  echo "bye"
} > ftp.txt
```

Test As You Go

Rather than save all the debugging until the end, it should be an integral part of the process of developing a program. Each section should be tested as it is written. As an example, we'll look at a function I wrote as part of a chess program. No, it's not a chess-playing program (though it could be when it's completed); that would be excruciatingly slow in the shell. It's a set of functions for preparing instructional material.

It needs to be able to convert one form of chess notation to another and to list all possible moves for any piece on the board. It needs to be able to tell whether a move is legal and to create a new board position after a move has been made. At its most basic level, it has to be able to convert a square in standard algebraic notation (SAN) to its numeric rank and file. That's what this function does.

The SAN format for naming a square is a lowercase letter representing the file and a number representing the rank. Files are rows of squares from white's side of the board to black's. Ranks are rows of squares from left to right. The square in white's left-hand corner is a1; that in black's is h8. To calculate possible moves, these need to be converted to the rank and file: a1 is converted to rank=1 and file=1; h8 becomes rank=8 and file=8.

It's a simple function, but it demonstrates how to test a function. The function receives the name of a square as an argument and stores the rank and file in those variables. If the square is not valid, it sets both rank and file to 0 and returns an error.

```
split_square() #@ DESCRIPTION: convert SAN square to numeric rank and file
{                  #@ USAGE: split_square SAN-SQUARE
  local square=$1
  rank=${square#?}
  case $square in
    a[1-8]) file=1;; ## Conversion of file to number
    b[1-8]) file=2;; ## and checking that the rank is
    c[1-8]) file=3;; ## a valid number are done in a
    d[1-8]) file=4;; ## single look-up
    e[1-8]) file=5;;
    f[1-8]) file=6;; ## If the rank is not valid,
    g[1-8]) file=7;; ## it falls through to the default
    h[1-8]) file=8;;
    *) file=0
       rank=0
       return 1      ## Not a valid square
       ;;
  esac
  return 0
}
```

To test this function, it is passed all possible legitimate squares as well as some that are not. It prints the name of the square and the file and rank numbers.

```
test_split_square()
{
  local f r
  for f in {a..i}
  do
    for r in {1..9}
    do
      split_square "$f$r"
      printf "$f$r %d-%d   " "$file" "$rank"
    done
    echo
  done
}
```

When the test is run, the output is as follows:

```
a1 1-1  a2 1-2  a3 1-3  a4 1-4  a5 1-5  a6 1-6  a7 1-7  a8 1-8  a9 0-0
b1 2-1  b2 2-2  b3 2-3  b4 2-4  b5 2-5  b6 2-6  b7 2-7  b8 2-8  b9 0-0
c1 3-1  c2 3-2  c3 3-3  c4 3-4  c5 3-5  c6 3-6  c7 3-7  c8 3-8  c9 0-0
d1 4-1  d2 4-2  d3 4-3  d4 4-4  d5 4-5  d6 4-6  d7 4-7  d8 4-8  d9 0-0
e1 5-1  e2 5-2  e3 5-3  e4 5-4  e5 5-5  e6 5-6  e7 5-7  e8 5-8  e9 0-0
f1 6-1  f2 6-2  f3 6-3  f4 6-4  f5 6-5  f6 6-6  f7 6-7  f8 6-8  f9 0-0
g1 7-1  g2 7-2  g3 7-3  g4 7-4  g5 7-5  g6 7-6  g7 7-7  g8 7-8  g9 0-0
h1 8-1  h2 8-2  h3 8-3  h4 8-4  h5 8-5  h6 8-6  h7 8-7  h8 8-8  h9 0-0
i1 0-0  i2 0-0  i3 0-0  i4 0-0  i5 0-0  i6 0-0  i7 0-0  i8 0-0  i9 0-0
```

All squares with the rank and file 0-0 are invalid.

Debugging a Script

In the wfe script, which was presented section by section earlier, there are a few bugs. Let's run that script and see what happens. The script is in $HOME/bin, which is in your PATH, and it can therefore be called by its name alone. Before that, however, a good first step is to check the script with the -n option. This tests for any syntax errors without actually executing the code:

```
$ bash -n wfe
/home/chris/bin/wfe-sh: wfe: line 70: unexpected EOF while looking for matching `"'
/home/chris/bin/wfe-sh: wfe: line 72: syntax error: unexpected end of file
```

The error message says that there's a missing quotation mark ("). It has reached the end of the file without finding it. That means it could be missing anywhere in the file. After a quick (or not-so-quick) glance through the file, it's not apparent where it should be.

When that happens, I start removing sections from the bottom of the file until the error disappears. I remove the last section; it's still there. I remove the option parsing, and the error hasn't disappeared. I remove the last function definition, version(), and the error has gone. The error must be in that function; where is it?

```
version() #@ DESCRIPTION: print script's version information
{         #@ USAGE: version
          #@ REQUIRES: variables defined: $scriptname, $author and $version
  printf "%s version %s\n" "$scriptname" "$version"
  printf "by %s, %d\n" "$author"  "${date_of_creation%%-*"
}
```

There are no mismatched quotations marks, so some other closing character must be missing and causing the problem. After a quick look, I see that the last variable expansion is missing a closing brace. Fixed, it becomes "${date_of_creation%%-*}". Another check with -n, and it gets a clean bill of health. Now it's time to run it:

```
$ wfe
bash: /home/chris/bin/wfe: Permission denied
```

Oops! We forgot to make the script executable. This doesn't usually happen with a main script; it happens more often with scripts that are called by another script. Change the permissions and try again:

```
$ chmod +x /home/chris/bin/wfe
$ wfe
cat: /home/chris/singlewords: No such file or directory
```

Have you downloaded the two files, singlewords and Compounds? If so, where did you put them? In the script, they are declared to be in $dict, which is defined as $HOME. If you put them somewhere else, such as in a subdirectory named words, change that line in the script. Let's make a directory, words, and put them in there:

```
mkdir $HOME/words &&
cd $HOME/words &&
wget http://cfaj.freeshell.org/wordfinder/singlewords &&
wget http://cfaj.freeshell.org/wordfinder/Compounds
```

In the script, change the assignment of dict to reflect the actual location of these files:

```
dict=$HOME/words
```

Let's try again:

```
$ wfe
a
aa
Aachen
aalii
aardvark
.... 183,758 words skipped ....
zymotic
zymotically
zymurgy
Zyrian
zythum
```

We forgot to tell the program what we are searching for. The script ought to have checked that an argument was supplied, but we forgot to include a sanity check section. Add that before the search is done (after the line shift $(($OPTIND - 1))).

```
## Check that user entered a search term
if [ -z "$pattern" ]
then
  {
    echo "Search term missing"
    usage
  } >&2
  exit 1
fi
```

Now, try again:

```
$ wfe
Search term missing
wfe - List words ending with REGEX
USAGE: wfe [-c|-h|-v] REGEX
```

That's better. Now let's really look for some words:

```
$ wfe drow
a
aa
Aachen
aalii
aardvark
.... 183,758 words skipped ....
zymotic
zymotically
```

```
zymurgy
Zyrian
zythum
```

There's still something wrong.

One of the most useful debugging tools is set -x, which prints each command with its expanded arguments as it is executed. Each line is preceded by the value of the PS4 variable. The default value of PS4 is "+ "; we'll change it to include the number of the line being executed. Put these two lines before the final section of the script:

```
export PS4='+ $LINENO: ' ## single quotes prevent $LINENO being expanded immediately
set -x
```

and try again:

```
$ wfe drow
++ 77: cat /home/chris/singlewords
++ 82: grep -i '.$'
++ 83: sort -fu
++ 78: '[' -n '' ']' ## Ctrl-C pressed to stop entire word list being printed
```

On line 82, you see that the pattern entered on the command line is missing. How did that happen? It should be grep -i '.drow$'. Line 82 in the script is as follows:

```
} | grep -i ".$regex$" |
```

What happened to the value of regex? Comment out set -x, and add the set -u option at the top of the script. This option treats unset variables as an error when they are expanded. Run the script again to check whether regex is set.

```
$ wfe drow
/home/chris/bin/wfe: line 84: regex: unbound variable
```

Why is regex unset? Take a look earlier in the script and see what variable was used to hold the command-line argument. Oh! It was pattern, not regex. You have to be consistent, and regex is a better description of its contents, so let's use that. Change all instances of pattern to regex. You should do it in the comments at the top, as well. Now try it.

```
$ wfe drow
windrow
```

Success! Now add compound words and phrases to the mix with the -c option:

```
$ wfe -c drow
/home/chris/bin/wfe: line 58: compoundfile: unbound variable
```

Here we go again! Surely we assigned the Compounds file in the *file locations* section. Take a look; yes, it's there on line 23 or thereabouts. Wait a minute, there's a typo: conpoundfile=$dict/Compounds. Change con to com. Keep your fingers crossed.

```
$ wfe -c drow
$
```

What? Nothing? Not even `windrow`? It's time to set `-x` and see what's going on. Uncomment that line, and play it again.

```
$ wfe -c drow
++ 79: cat /home/chris/singlewords
++ 84: grep -i '.-c$'
++ 85: sort -fu
++ 80: '[' -n /home/chris/Compounds ']'
++ 82: cut -f1 /home/chris/Compounds
```

At least that's easy to figure out. We assigned `regex` before processing the options, and it snarfed the first argument, the `-c` option. Move the assignment down to after the `getopts` section, specifically, to after the `shift` command. (And you'll probably want to comment out set `-x`.)

```
shift $(( $OPTIND - 1 ))

## Regular expression supplied on the command line
regex=$1
```

Are there any more issues?

```
$ wfe -c drow
skidRow
windrow
```

That looks good. It might seem like a lot of work for a small script, but it seems longer in the telling than in the doing, especially once you get used to doing it—or, better still, getting it right in the first place.

Summary

Bugs are inevitable, but with care, most can be prevented. When they do materialize, there are shell options to help trace the problem.

Exercises

1. What is wrong with `if [ $var=x ]`? What should it be? Why does it give the result it does?

2. Write a function, `valid_square()`, that returns successfully if its sole argument is a valid SAN chessboard square or fails if it is not. Write a function to test that it works.

■ ■ ■

## CHAPTER 11

Programming for the Command Line

This book is about programming with the shell, not about using it at the command line. You will not find information about editing the command line, creating a command prompt (the PS1 variable), or retrieving commands from your interactive history. This chapter is about scripts that will mostly be useful at the command line rather than in other scripts.

Many of the scripts in this chapter are shell functions. Some of them have to be that way because they change the environment. Others are functions because they are often used and are quicker that way. Others are both functions and stand-alone scripts.

Manipulating the Directory Stack

The cd command remembers the previous working directory, and cd - will return to it. There is another command that will change the directory and will remember an unlimited number of directories: pushd. The directories are stored in an array, DIRSTACK. To return to a previous directory, popd pulls the top entry off DIRSTACK and makes that the current directory. I use two functions that make handling DIRSTACK easier, and I've added a third one here just for the sake of completeness.

cd

The cd function replaces the builtin command of the same name. The function uses the builtin command pushd to change the directory and store the new directory on DIRSTACK. If no directory is given, pushd uses $HOME. If changing the directory fails, cd prints an error message, and the function returns with a failing exit code (see Listing 11-1).

Listing 11-1. cd, Change Directory, Saving Location on the Directory Stack

```
cd() #@ Change directory, storing new directory on DIRSTACK
{
  local dir error       ## variables for directory and return code

  while :                ## ignore all options
  do
    case $1 in
      --) break ;;
      -*) shift ;;
```

```
      *) break ;;
    esac
  done

  dir=$1

  if [ -n "$dir" ]        ## if a $dir is not empty
  then
    pushd "$dir"          ## change directory
  else
    pushd "$HOME"         ## go HOME if nothing on the command line
  fi 2>/dev/null          ## error message should come from cd, not pushd

  error=$?      ## store pushd's exit code

  if [ $error -ne 0 ]     ## failed, print error message
  then
    builtin cd "$dir"     ## let the builtin cd provide the error message
  fi
  return "$error"         ## leave with pushd's exit code
} > /dev/null
```

The standard output is redirected to the bit bucket because pushd prints the contents of DIRSTACK, and the only other output is sent to standard error (>&2).

■ **Note** A replacement for a standard command such as cd should accept anything that the original accepts. In the case of cd, the options -L and -P are accepted, even though they are ignored. That said, I do sometimes ignore options without even making provisions for them, especially if they are ones I never use.

---

pd

This function is here for the sake of completeness (see Listing 11-2). It is a lazy man's way of calling popd; I don't use it.

Listing 11-2. pd, Return to Previous Directory with popd

```
pd ()
{
    popd
} >/dev/null ### for the same reason as cd
```

cdm

The reason I don't use pd is not that I'm not lazy. Far from it, but I prefer to leave DIRSTACK intact so that I can move back and forth between directories. For that, I use a menu that presents all the directories in DIRSTACK.

The cdm function sets the Input Field Separator (IFS) to a single newline (NL or LF) to ensure that the output of the dirs builtin command keeps file names together after word splitting (Listing 11-3). File names containing a newline would still cause problems; names with spaces are an annoyance, but names with newlines are an abomination.

The function loops through the names in DIRSTACK (for dir in $(dirs -l -p)) adding each one to an array, item, unless it is already there. This array is then used as the arguments to the menu function (discussed in a moment), which must be sourced before cdm can be used.

DIRS BUILTIN COMMAND

The dirs builtin command lists the directories in the DIRSTACK array. By default, it lists them on a single line with the value of HOME represented by a tilde. The -l option expands ~ to $HOME, and -p prints the directories one per line.

Listing 11-3. cdm, Select New Directory from a Menu of Those Already Visited

```
cdm() #@ select new directory from a menu of those already visited
{
  local dir IFS=$'\n' item
  for dir in $(dirs -l -p)                ## loop through diretories in DIRSTACK[@]
  do
    [ "$dir" = "$PWD" ] && continue     ## skip current directory
    case ${item[*]} in
      *"$dir:"*) ;;                     ## $dir already in array; do nothing
      *) item+=( "$dir:cd '$dir'" ) ;;  ## add $dir to array
    esac
  done
  menu "${item[@]}" Quit:                ## pass array to menu function
}
```

When run, the menu looks like this:

```
$ cdm

    1. /public/music/magnatune.com
    2. /public/video
    3. /home/chris
    4. /home/chris/tmp/qwe rty uio p
    5. /home/chris/tmp
    6. Quit

 (1 to 6) ==>
```

menu

The calling syntax for this menu function comes from 9menu, which was part of the Plan 9 operating system. Each argument contains two colon-separated fields: the item to be displayed and the command to be executed. If there is no colon in an argument, it is used both as the display and as the command:

```
$ menu who date "df:df ."

    1. who
    2. date
    3. df

 (1 to 3) ==> 3
Filesystem           1K-blocks        Used Available Use% Mounted on
/dev/hda5             48070472    43616892   2011704  96% /home
$ menu who date "df: df ."

    1. who
    2. date
    3. df

 (1 to 3) ==> 1
chris     tty8         Jun 18 14:00 (:1)
chris     tty2         Jun 21 18:10
```

A for loop numbers and prints the menu; read gets the response; and a case statement checks for the exit characters q, Q, or 0 in the response. Finally, indirect expansion retrieves the selected item, further expansion extracts the command, and eval executes it: eval "${!num#*:}" (Listing 11-4).

Listing 11-4. menu, Print Menu and Execute Associated Command

```
menu()
{
  local IFS=$' \t\n'                       ## Use default setting of IFS
  local num n=1 opt item cmd
  echo

  ## Loop though the command-line arguments
  for item
  do
    printf "  %3d. %s\n" "$n" "${item%%:*}"
    n=$(( $n + 1 ))
  done
  echo

  ## If there are fewer than 10 items, set option to accept key without ENTER
  if [ $# -lt 10 ]
  then
    opt=-sn1
  else
    opt=
```

```
  fi
  read -p " (1 to $#) ==> " $opt num          ## Get response from user

  ## Check that user entry is valid
  case $num in
    [qQ0] | "" ) return ;;                    ## q, Q or 0 or "" exits
    *[!0-9]* | 0*)                            ## invalid entry
        printf "\aInvalid response: %s\n" "$num" >&2
        return 1
        ;;
  esac
  echo

  if [ "$num" -le "$#" ]   ## Check that number is <= to the number of menu items
  then
    eval "${!num#*:}"       ## Execute it using indirect expansion
  else
    printf "\aInvalid response: %s\n" "$num" >&2
    return 1
  fi
}
```

Filesystem Functions

These functions vary from laziness (giving a short name to a longer command) to adding functionality to standard commands (cp and mv). They list, copy, or move files or create directories.

l

There is no single-letter command required by the POSIX specification, and there is only one that is found on most Unixes: w, which shows who is logged on and what they are doing. I have defined a number of single-letter functions:

- a: Lists the currently playing music track

- c: Clears the screen (sometimes quicker or easier than ^L)

- d: date "+%A, %-d %B %Y %-I:%M:%S %P (%H:%M:%S)"

- k: Is equivalent to man -k, or apropos

- t: For the Amiga and MS-DOS command type, invokes less

- v and V: Lowers and raises the sound volume, respectively

- x: logout

And there's the one I use most that pipes a long file listing through less, shown in Listing 11-5.

Listing 11-5. 1, List Files in Long Format, Piped Through less

```
l()
{
  ls -lA "$@" | less       ## the -A option is specific to GNU and *BSD versions
}
```

lsr

The commands I use most frequently are l, cd, xx.sh, cdm, and lsr. xx.sh is a file for throwaway scripts. I keep adding new ones to the top; lsr displays the most recent files (or with the -o option, the oldest files). The default setting is for ten files to be shown, but that can be changed with the -n option.

The script in Listing 11-6 uses the -t (or -tr) option to ls and pipes the result to head.

Listing 11-6. 1sr, List Most Recently Modified Files

```
num=10                                      ## number of files to print
short=0                                     ## set to 1 for short listing
timestyle='--time-style="+ %d-%b-%Y %H:%M:%S "'  ## GNU-specific time format

opts=Aadn:os

while getopts $opts opt
do
  case $opt in
      a|A|d) ls_opts="$ls_opts -$opt" ;;  ## options passed to ls
      n) num=$OPTARG ;;                   ## number of files to display
      o) ls_opts="$ls_opts -r" ;;         ## show oldest files, not newest
      s) short=$(( $short + 1 )) ;;
  esac
done
shift $(( $OPTIND - 1 ))

case $short in
    0) ls_opts="$ls_opts -l -t" ;;        ## long listing, use -l
    *) ls_opts="$ls_opts -t" ;;           ## short listing, do not use -l
esac

ls $ls_opts $timestyle "$@" | {
    read                                  ## In bash, the same as: IFS= read -r REPLY
    case $line in
        total*) ;;                        ## do not display the 'total' line
        *) printf "%s\n" "$REPLY" ;;
    esac
    cat
} | head -n$num
```

cp, mv

Before switching my desktop to GNU/Linux, I used an Amiga. Its copy command would copy a file to the current directory if no destination was given. This function gives the same ability as cp (Listing 11-7). The -b option is GNU specific, so remove it if you are using a different version of cp.

Listing 11-7. cp, Copy, Using the Current Directory If No Destination Is Given

```
cp()
{
  local final
  if [ $# -eq 1 ]                ## Only one arg,
  then
    command cp -b "$1" .         ## so copy it to the current directory
  else
    final=${!#}
    if [ -d "$final" ]           ## if last arg is a directory
    then
      command cp -b "$@"         ## copy all the files into it
    else
      command cp -b "$@" .       ## otherwise, copy to the current directory
    fi
  fi
}
```

The mv function is identical except that it has mv wherever cp appears in that function.

md

Laziness is the order of the day with the md function (Listing 11-8). It calls mkdir with the -p option to create intermediate directories if they don't exist. With the -c option, md creates the directory (if it doesn't already exist) and then cds into it. Because of the -p option, no error is generated if the directory exists.

Listing 11-8. md, Create a New Directory and Intermediate Directories and Optionally cd into It

```
md() { #@ create new directory, including intermediate directories if necessary
  case $1 in
    -c) mkdir -p "$2" && cd "$2" ;;
    *) mkdir -p "$@" ;;
  esac
}
```

Miscellaneous Functions

I use the next two functions a great deal, but they don't fit into any category.

pr1

I have the pr1 function as both a function and a stand-alone script (Listing 11-9). It prints each of its argument on a separate line. By default, it limits the length to the number of columns in the terminal, truncating lines as necessary.

There are two options, -w and -W. The former removes the truncation, so lines will always print in full, wrapping to the next line when necessary. The latter specifies a width at which to truncate lines.

Listing 11-9. pr1, Function to Print Its Argument One to a Line

```
pr1() #@ Print arguments one to a line
{
  case $1 in
    -w) pr_w=                    ## width specification modifier
        shift
        ;;
    -W) pr_w=${2}
        shift 2
        ;;
    -W*) pr_w=${1#??}
        shift
        ;;
    *) pr_w=-.${COLUMNS:-80}     ## default to number of columns in window
        ;;
  esac
  printf "%${pr_w}s\n" "$@"
}
```

The script version uses getopts; I didn't use them in the function because I wanted it to be POSIX compliant (Listing 11-10).

Listing 11-10. pr1, Script to Print Its Arguments One to a Line

```
while getopts wW: opt
do
  case $opt in
    w) w=
       shift
       ;;
```

```
    W) w=$OPTARG ;;
    *) w=-.${COLUMNS:-80} ;;
  esac
done
shift $(( $OPTIND - 1 ))

printf "%${w}s\n" "$@"
```

calc

Bash lacks the capacity for arithmetic with decimal fractions, so I wrote this function (Listing 11-11) to use awk to do the dirty work. Note that characters special to the shell must be escaped or quoted on the command line. This applies particularly to the multiplication symbol, *.

Listing 11-11. calc, Print Result of Arithmetic Expression

```
calc() #@ Perform arithmetic, including decimal fractions
{
  local result=$(awk 'BEGIN { OFMT="%f"; print '"$*"'; exit}')
  case $result in
    *.*0) result=${result%"${result##*[!0]}"} ;;
  esac
  printf "%s\n" "$result"
}
```

The case statement removes trailing zeroes after a decimal point.

Managing Man Pages

I use three functions related to man pages. The first searches a man page for a pattern or string, the second looks up a POSIX man page, and the third is equivalent to man -k.

sman

This function calls up a man page and searches for a given string. It assumes that less is the default pager (Listing 11-12).

Listing 11-12. sman, Call Up a Man Page and Search for a Pattern

```
sman() #@ USAGE: sman command search_pattern
{
  LESS="$LESS${2:+ +/$2}" man "$1"
}
```

sus

When I want to check the portability of a given command or, more usually, to check which options are specified by POSIX, I use sus. It stores a copy of the POSIX man page locally so that it doesn't need to be fetched on subsequent queries (Listing 11-13).

Listing 11-13. sus, Look Up a Man Page in the POSIX Spec

```
sus()
{
    local html_file=/usr/share/sus/$1.html    ## adjust to taste
    local dir=9699919799
    local sus_dir=http://www.opengroup.org/onlinepubs/$dir/utilities/
    [ -f "$html_file" ] ||
      lynx -source $sus_dir${1##*/}.html > $html_file ##>/dev/null 2>&1
    lynx -dump -nolist $html_file | ${PAGER:-less}
}
```

lynx is a text-mode web browser. Though normally used interactively to access the Web, the -source and -dump directives can be used in scripts.

k

This function saves all the typing of apropos or man -k. It actually does a little more. It filters the result so that only user commands (from the first section of the man pages) show. System and kernel functions and file specifications, and so on, do not get shown (Listing 11-14).

Listing 11-14. k, List Commands Whose Short Descriptions Include a Search String

```
k() #@ USAGE: k string
{
    man -k "$@" | grep '(1'
}
```

Games

What's a command line without games? Boring, that's what! I have written a number of games using the shell. They include yahtzee (Figure 11-1), a game that uses five dice; maxit (Figure 11-2), based on an arithmetic game for the Commodore 64; and, of course, tic-tac-toe (Figure 11-3). All these games are too large to include in this book, but sections of them (such as the yahtzee dice) will be demonstrated in later chapters. The one game that I can include here is the fifteen puzzle.

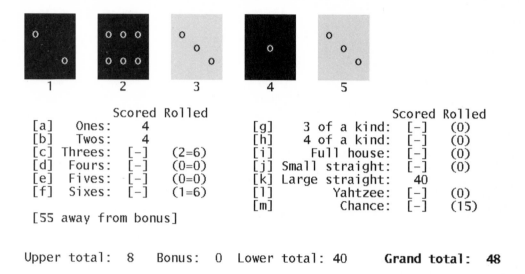

```
                Scored Rolled                        Scored Rolled
[a]    Ones:      4               [g]    3 of a kind:  [-]   (0)
[b]    Twos:      4               [h]    4 of a kind:  [-]   (0)
[c]  Threes:    [-]   (2=6)       [i]     Full house:  [-]   (0)
[d]   Fours:    [-]   (0=0)       [j] Small straight:  [-]   (0)
[e]   Fives:    [-]   (0=0)       [k] Large straight:   40
[f]   Sixes:    [-]   (1=6)       [l]        Yahtzee:  [-]   (0)
                                  [m]         Chance:  [-]   (15)
[55 away from bonus]
```

```
Upper total:  8   Bonus:  0  Lower total: 40   Grand total:  48
```

Figure 11-1. The game of yahtzee, in which the player attempts to get runs, a full house, or three/four/five of a kind

```
H:           human:  43  (last=   4)
V:            max1:  29  (last=   4)
Points left: -96

 --- --- --- --- --- --- --- ---
| -4| 13| -6|  8| -6|  1| -9|  1|
 --- --- --- --- --- --- --- ---
| -1| -2|  7|  9| -6| -7|  1| -1|
===============================
| -6| -4| -7| 13|    2|  7| -6|
===============================
|   | -5|  4| -2|-10|   | -9|   |
 --- --- --- --- --- --- --- ---
|  3| 11| -1|  0|  2|   |  1|   |
 --- --- --- --- --- --- --- ---
|   |-12|-13| -6|   | -2| -5|-13|
 --- --- --- --- --- --- --- ---
|-15| -8| 11|  0|  1| -6| 13| -8|
 --- --- --- --- --- --- --- ---
| 10| 10|-12|-12|  2|-14| -1| -7|
 --- --- --- --- --- --- --- ---
```

Figure 11-2. The game of maxit, in which one player selects from a row, and the other from a column

```
  O |   | X
---+---+---
  O | O | X
---+---+---
  X |   |
```

Select (2 8 9): ▊

Figure 11-3. The ubiquitous game of tic-tac-toe

The Fifteen Puzzle

The fifteen puzzle consists of 15 numbered, sliding tiles in a frame; the object is to arrange them in ascending order like this:

In this script (Listing 11-15), the tiles are moved with the cursor keys.

Listing 11-15. fifteen, *Place Tiles in Ascending Order*

```
########################################
## Meta data
########################################

scriptname=${0##*/}
description="The Fifteen Puzzle"
author="Chris F.A. Johnson"
created=2009-06-20
```

```
########################################
## Variables
########################################

board=( {1..15} "" )      ## The basic board array
target=( "${board[@]}" )   ## A copy for comparison (the target)
empty=15                   ## The empty square
last=0                     ## The last move made
A=0 B=1 C=2 D=3            ## Indices into array of possible moves
topleft='\e[0;0H'          ## Move cursor to top left corner of window
nocursor='\e[?25l'         ## Make cursor invisible
normal=\e[0m\e[?12l\e[?25h ## Resume normal operation

## Board layout is a printf format string
## At its most basic, it could be a simple:

fmt="$nocursor$topleft


    %2s  %2s  %2s  %2s

    %2s  %2s  %2s  %2s

    %2s  %2s  %2s  %2s

    %2s  %2s  %2s  %2s

"

## I prefer this ASCII board
fmt="\e[?25l\e[0;0H\n
\t+----+----+----+----+
\t|    |    |    |    |
\t| %2s | %2s | %2s | %2s |
\t|    |    |    |    |
\t+----+----+----+----+
\t|    |    |    |    |
\t| %2s | %2s | %2s | %2s |
\t|    |    |    |    |
\t+----+----+----+----+
\t|    |    |    |    |
\t| %2s | %2s | %2s | %2s |
\t|    |    |    |    |
\t+----+----+----+----+
\t|    |    |    |    |
\t| %2s | %2s | %2s | %2s |
\t|    |    |    |    |
\t+----+----+----+----+\n\n"
```

```
#######################################
###  Functions
#######################################

print_board() #@ What the name says
{
    printf "$fmt" "${board[@]}"
}

borders() #@ List squares bordering on the empty square
{
    ## Calculate x/y co-ordinates of the empty square
    local x=$(( ${empty:=0} % 4 ))  y=$(( $empty / 4 ))

    ## The array, bordering, has 4 elements, corresponding to the 4 directions
    ## If a move in any direction would be off the board, that element is empty
    ##
    unset bordering       ## clear array before setting it
    [ $y -lt 3 ] && bordering[$A]=$(( $empty + 4 ))
    [ $y -gt 0 ] && bordering[$B]=$(( $empty - 4 ))
    [ $x -gt 0 ] && bordering[$C]=$(( $empty - 1 ))
    [ $x -lt 3 ] && bordering[$D]=$(( $empty + 1 ))
}

check() #@ Check whether puzzle has been solved
{
    ## Compare current board with target
    if [ "${board[*]}" = "${target[*]}" ]
    then
        ## Puzzle is completed, print message and exit
        print_board
        printf "\a\tCompleted in %d moves\n\n"  "$moves"
        exit
    fi
}

move() #@ Move the square in $1
{
    movelist="$empty $movelist"    ## add current empty square to the move list
    moves=$(( $moves + 1 ))        ## increment move counter
    board[$empty]=${board[$1]}     ## put $1 into the current empty square
    board[$1]=""                   ## remove number from new empty square
    last=$empty                    ## .... and put it in old empty square
    empty=$1                       ## set new value for empty-square pointer
}

random_move() #@ Move one of the squares in the arguments
{
    ## The arguments to random_move are the squares that can be moved
    ## (as generated by the borders function)
    local sq
    while :
```

```
  do
    sq=$(( $RANDOM % $# + 1 ))
    sq=${!sq}
    [ $sq -ne ${last:-666} ] &&    ## do not undo last move
        break
  done
  move "$sq"
}

shuffle() #@ Mix up the board using legitimate moves (to ensure solvable puzzle)
{
  local n=0 max=$(( $RANDOM % 100 + 150 ))   ## number of moves to make
  while [ $(( n += 1 )) -lt $max ]
  do
    borders                                ## generate list of possible moves
    random_move "${bordering[@]}"          ## move to one of them at random
  done
}


#########################################
### End of functions
#########################################

trap 'printf "$normal"' EXIT               ## return terminal to normal state on exit


#########################################
### Instructions and initialization
#########################################

clear
print_board
echo
printf "\t%s\n" "$description" "by $author, ${created%%-*}" ""
printf "
 Use the cursor keys to move the tiles around.

 The game is finished when you return to the
 position shown above.

 Try to complete the puzzle in as few moves
 as possible.


        Press \e[1mENTER\e[0m to continue
"
shuffle                                 ## randomize board
moves=0                                 ## reset move counter
read -s                                 ## wait for user
clear                                   ## clear the screen
```

```
########################################
### Main loop
########################################

while :
do
  borders
  print_board
  printf "\t    %d move" "$moves"
  [ $moves -ne 1 ] && printf "s"
  check

  ## read a single character without waiting for <ENTER>
  read -sn1 -p $'         \e[K' key

  ## The cursor keys generate three characters: ESC, [ and A, B, C, or D;
  ## this loop will run three times for each press of a cursor key
  ## but will not do anything until it receives a letter
  ## from the cursor key (or entered directly with A etc.), or a 'q' to exit
  case $key in
    A) [ -n "${bordering[$A]}" ] && move "${bordering[$A]}" ;;
    B) [ -n "${bordering[$B]}" ] && move "${bordering[$B]}" ;;
    C) [ -n "${bordering[$C]}" ] && move "${bordering[$C]}" ;;
    D) [ -n "${bordering[$D]}" ] && move "${bordering[$D]}" ;;
    q) echo; break ;;
  esac
done
```

Summary

These 15 scripts provided a smattering of the possibilities for using scripts at the command line. Where the environment needs to be changed (as in cd and cdm), the scripts must be shell functions. These are usually kept in $HOME/.bashrc or in a file sourced by .bashrc.

Even games can be programmed without needing a GUI interface.

Exercises

1. Modify the menu function to accept its parameters from a file.

2. Rewrite the pr1 function as prx that will behave in the manner of pr4 from Chapter 8 but will take an option for any number of columns.

3. Add a getopts section to the fifteen game that allows the user to select between three different board formats. Write a third format.

CHAPTER 12

■ ■ ■

Runtime Configuration

When I download my mail from three or four different POP3 servers, I don't use a different script for each one. When I open a terminal to ssh to a remote computer (half a dozen of them) with a different background color for each, I use the same script for every connection. To upload files to my web sites (I look after six sites), I use the same script for all of them.

You can configure a script's behavior in several ways when you run it. This chapter looks at seven methods: initialized variables, command-line options and arguments, menus, Q&A dialogue, configuration files, multiple names for one script, and environment variables. These methods are not mutually exclusive; in fact, they are often combined. A command-line option could tell the script to use a different configuration file or present the user with a menu.

Defining Variables

If the runtime requirements for a script rarely change, hard-coded variables may be all the configuration you need (Listing 12-1). You can set them when the script is installed. When a change *is* needed, the parameters can quickly be changed with a text editor.

Listing 12-1. Example of Initialized Default Variables

```
## File locations
dict=/usr/share/dict
wordfile=$dict/singlewords
compoundfile=$dict/Compounds

## Default is not to show compound words
compounds=no
```

If the variables need changing often, one or more of the other methods can be added.

Command-Line Options and Arguments

The most common method for changing runtime behavior uses command-line options. As shown in Listing 12-2, all the values defined earlier can be modified at the command line.

Listing 12-2. Parse Command-Line Options

```
while getopts d:w:f:c var
do
  case "$var" in
    c) compounds=1 ;;
    d) dict=$OPTARG ;;
    w) wordfile=$OPTARG ;;
    f) compoundfile=$OPTARG ;;
  esac
done
```

Menus

For a user unfamiliar with a piece of software, a menu is a good way to allow runtime changes. In the menu example shown in Listing 12-3, the selections are numbered from 1 to 4, and q exits the menu.

Listing 12-3. Set Parameters via Menu

```
while :   ## loop until user presses 'q'
do
  ## print menu
  printf "\n\n%s\n" "$bar"
  printf "  Dictionary parameters\n"
  printf "%s\n\n" "$bar"
  printf "  1. Directory containing dictionary: %s\n" "$dict"
  printf "  2. File containing word list: %s\n" "$wordfile"
  printf "  3. File containing compound words and phrases: %s\n" "$compoundfile"
  printf "  4. Include compound words and phrases in results? %s\n" "$compounds"
  printf "  q. %s\n" "Exit menu"
  printf "\n%s\n\n" "$bar"

  ## get user response
  read -sn1 -p "Select (1,2,3,4,q): " input
  echo

  ## interpret user response
  case $input in
    1) read -ep "Enter dictionary directory: " dict ;;
    2) read -ep "Enter word-list file: " wordfile ;;
    3) read -ep "Enter compound-word file: " compoundfile ;;
    4) [ "$compounds" = y ] && compounds=n || compounds=y ;;
    q) break ;;
    *) printf "\n\aInvalid selection: %c\n" "$input" >&2
    sleep 2
    ;;
  esac
done
```

Q&A Dialogue

A question-and-answer function cycles through all the parameters, prompting the user to enter a value for each one (Listing 12-4). This can get tedious for the user, and it is probably best used when there are no defaults, when there are very few parameters to enter, or when values need to be entered for a new configuration file.

Listing 12-4. Set Variables by Question and Answer

```
read -ep "Directory containing dictionary: " dict
read -ep "File containing word list: " wordfile
read -ep "File containing compound words and phrases: " compoundfile
read -sn1 -p "Include compound words and phrases in results (y/n)? " compounds
echo
read -ep "Save parameters (y/n)? " save
case $save in
  y|Y) read -ep "Enter path to configuration file: " configfile
    {
    printf '%-30s ## %s"\n' \
       "dict=$dict" "Directory containing dictionary" \
       "wordfile=$wordfile" "File containing word list" \
       "compoundfile=$compoundfile" "File containing compound words and phrases" \
       "Compounds" "$Compounds" "Include compound words and phrases in results?"
    } > "${configfile:-/dev/tty}"
esac
```

Configuration Files

Configuration files can use any format, but it's easiest to make them shell scripts that can be sourced. The example file shown in Listing 12-5 can be sourced, but it can also provide more information.

Listing 12-5. Configuration File, words.cfg

```
dict=/usr/share/dict        ## directory containing dictionary files
wordfile=singlewords        ## file containing word list
compoundfile=Compounds      ## file containing compound words and phrases
compounds=no                ## include compound words and phrases in results?
```

The words.cfg file can be sourced with either of these two commands:

```
. words.cfg
source words.cfg
```

Rather than sourcing the file, it can be parsed in various ways (Listing 12-6). In bash-4.0, you can read the file into an array and extract the variables and comments using *parameter expansion*, the expansion being applied to each element of the array.

Listing 12-6. Parsing Configuration File

```
IFS=$'\n'
file=words.cfg
settings=( $( < "$file") )          ## store file in array, 1 line per element
eval "${settings[@]%%#*}"           ## extract and execute the assignments
comments=( "${settings[@]#*## }" )  ## store comments in array
```

The comments array contains just the comments, and the assignments can be extracted from settings with "${settings[@]%%#*}":

```
$ printf "%s\n" "${comments[@]}"
directory containing dictionary files
file containing word list
file containing compound words and phrases
include compound words and phrases in results?
```

You can also read the file in a loop to set the variables and provide information about the variables it contains by displaying the comments (Listing 12-7).

Listing 12-7. Parsing Configuration File with Comments

```
while read assignment x comment
do
  if [ -n "$assignment" ]
  then
    printf "%20s: %s\n" "${assignment#*=}"  "$comment"
    eval "$assignment"
  fi
done < "$file"
```

The following is the result:

```
/usr/share/dict: directory containing dictionary files
    singlewords: file containing word list
      Compounds: file containing compound words and phrases
              n: include compound words and phrases in results?
```

Configuration files can be made as complex as you like, but parsing them then falls more properly under the category of data processing, which is the subject of the next chapter.

Scripts with Several Names

By storing the same file under different names, you can avoid command-line options and menus. The script in Listing 12-8 opens a terminal and connects to different remote computers using a secure shell. The terminal's colors, the machine to log on to, and the name of the remote user are all determined by the name of the script.

Listing 12-8. bashful, Connect to Remote Computer via ssh

```
scriptname=${0##*/}

## default colours
bg=#ffffcc      ## default background: pale yellow
fg=#000000      ## default foreground: black

user=bashful    ## default user name
term=xterm      ## default terminal emulator (I prefer rxvt)

case $scriptname in
  sleepy)
     bg=#ffffff
     user=sleepy
     host=sleepy.example.com
     ;;
  sneezy)
     fg=#aa0000
     bg=#ffeeee
     host=sneezy.example.org
     ;;
  grumpy)
     fg=#006600
     bg=#eeffee
     term=rxvt
     host=cfajohnson.example.com
     ;;
  dopey)
     host=127.0.0.1
     ;;
  *) echo "$scriptname: Unknown name" >&2
     exit 1
     ;;
esac

"$term" -fg "$fg" -bg "$bg" -e ssh -l "$user" "$host"
```

To create the multiple names for the same file, create links with ln (Listing 12-9).

Listing 12-9. Make Multiple Links to bashful Script

```
cd "$HOME/bin" &&
for name in sleepy sneezy grumpy dopey
do
  ln -s bashful "$name"            ## you can leave out the -s option if you like
done
```

Environment Variables

You can also pass settings to a program using variables. These can be either exported or defined on the same line as the command. In the latter case, the variable is defined for that command only.

You alter the behavior of the program by checking for the value of a variable or even just for its existence. I use this technique most often to adjust the output of a script using verbose. This would be a typical line in a script:

```
[ ${verbose:-0} -gt 0 ] && printf "%s\n" "Finished parsing options"
```

The script would be called with the following:

```
verbose=1 myscriptname
```

You can see an example in the following script.

All Together Now

The following is the program I use to update all my web sites. It finds new or modified files in a directory hierarchy, stores them in a tarball, and uploads them to a web site on a (usually) remote computer. I have shell access on all the sites I use, so I can use a secure shell, ssh, to transfer the files and unpack them with tar on the site:

```
ssh -p "$port" -l "$user" "$host" \
    "cd \"$dest\" || exit;tar -xpzf -" < "$tarfile" &&
        touch "$syncfile"
```

All of my sites use authentication keys (created with ssh-keygen) so that no password is required and so the script can be run as a cron job.

This program uses all the techniques mentioned earlier except for multiple names. It's more than you would usually use in a single program, but it's a good illustration.

The user can select whether to use command-line options, a menu, a Q&A dialogue, or a configuration file to adjust the settings, or the user can even use the defaults. Command-line options are available for all settings:

-c configfile: Reads settings from configfile

-h host: Specifies the URL or IP address of remote computer

-p port: Specifies the SSH port to use

-d dest: Specifies the destination directory on the remote host

-u user: Specifies the user's login name on remote computer

-a archivedir: Specifies the local directory to store archive files

-f syncfile: Specifies the file whose timestamp is the cut-off point
And there are three further options that control the script itself:

-t: Tests only, displays final settings, does not archive or upload

-m: Presents user with the menu

-q: Uses Q&A dialogue

The script is examined in the following sections in detail, section by section.

Script Information

Note that parameter expansion is used to pull the script name from $0, not the external command, basename (Listing 12-10).

Listing 12-10. upload, Archive and Upload Files to Remote Computer

```
scriptname=${0##*/}
description="Archive new or modified files and upload to web site"
author="Chris F.A. Johnson"
version=1.0
```

Default Configuration

Besides setting the variables, an array containing the names of the variables and their descriptions is created (Listing 12-10a). This is used by the menu and qa (question and answer) functions for labels and prompts.

Listing 12-10a. Default Values and settings Array

```
## archive and upload settings
host=127.0.0.1                         ## Remote host (URL or IP address)
port=22                                ## SSH port
dest=work/upload                       ## Destination directory
user=chris                             ## Login name on remote system
source=$HOME/public_html/example.com   ## Local directory to upload
archivedir=$HOME/work/webarchives      ## Directory to store archive files
syncfile=.sync                         ## File to touch with time of last upload

## array containing variables and their descriptions
varinfo=( "" ## Empty element to emulate 1-based array
  "host:Remote host (URL or IP address)"
  "port:SSH port"
  "dest:Destination directory"
  "user:Login name on remote system"
  "source:Local directory to upload"
  "archivedir:Directory to store archive files"
  "syncfile:File to touch with time of last upload"
)
```

```
## These may be changed by command-line options
menu=0          ## do not print a menu
qa=0            ## do not use question and answer
test=0          ## 0 = upload for real; 1 = don't archive/upload, show settings
configfile=     ## if defined, the file will be sourced
configdir=$HOME/.config  ## default location for configuration files
sleepytime=2    ## delay in seconds after printing messages

## Bar to print across top and bottom of menu (and possibly elsewhere)
bar=================================================================
bar=$bar$bar$bar$bar    ## make long enough for any terminal window
menuwidth=${COLUMNS:-80}
```

Screen Variables

These variables use the ISO-6429 standard, which is now all but universal in terminals and terminal emulators (Listing 12-10b). This is discussed in detail in Chapter 14. When printed to the terminal, these escape sequences perform the actions indicated in the comments.

Listing 12-10b. Define Screen Manipulation Variables

```
topleft='\e[0;0H'    ## Move cursor to top left corner of screen
clearEOS='\e[J'      ## Clear from cursor position to end of screen
clearEOL='\e[K'      ## Clear from cursor position to end of line
```

Function Definitions

There are five functions, two of which, menu and qa, allow the user to change the settings. With readline to accept the user's input, the -i option to read is used if the shell version is bash-4.0 or greater. If the test option is used, the print_config function outputs the settings in a format that is suitable for a configuration file, complete with comments.

Function: die

The program exits via the die function when a command fails (Listing 12-10c).

Listing 12-10c. Define die Function

```
die() #@ Print error message and exit with error code
{       #@ USAGE: die [errno [message]]

  error=${1:-1}    ## exits with 1 if error number not given
  shift
  [ -n "$*" ] &&
    printf "%s%s: %s\n" "$scriptname" ${version:+" ($version)"} "$*" >&2
  exit "$error"
}
```

Function: menu

The menu function uses its command-line arguments to populate the menu (Listing 12-10d). Each argument contains a variable name and a description of the variable separated by a colon.

THE UPLOAD SETTINGS MENU

```
=============================================================================
   UPLOAD SETTINGS
=============================================================================

   1: Remote host (URL or IP address) (127.0.0.1)
   2: ssh port (22)
   3: Destination directory (work/upload)
   4: Login name on remote system (chris)
   5: Local directory to upload (/home/chris/public_html/example.com)
   6: Directory to store archive files (/home/chris/work/webarchives)
   7: File to touch with time of last upload (.sync)
   q: Quit menu, start uploading
   0: Exit upload


=============================================================================

   Select 1..7 or 'q/0'
```

The function enters an infinite loop, from which the user exits by selecting q or 0. Within the loop, menu clears the screen and then cycles through each argument, storing it in item. It extracts the variable name and description using parameter expansion:

```
var=${item%%:*}
description=${item#*:}
```

The value of each var is obtained through indirect expansion, ${!var}, and is included in the menu labels.

The field width for the menu number is ${#max}, that is, the length of the highest item number.

Listing 12-10d. Define menu Function

```
menu() #@ Print menu, and change settings according to user input
{
  local max=$#
  local menutitle="UPLOAD SETTINGS"
  local readopt

  if [ $max -lt 10 ]
  then                  ## if fewer than ten items,
```

```
  readopt=-sn1    ## allow single key entry
else
  readopt=
fi

printf "$topleft$clearEOS"  ## Move to top left and clear screen

while : ## infinite loop
do

  #########################################################
  ## display menu
  ##
  printf "$topleft"  ## Move cursor to top left corner of screen

  ## print menu title between horizontal bars the width of the screen
  printf "\n%s\n" "${bar:0:$menuwidth}"
  printf "    %s\n" "$menutitle"
  printf "%s\n\n" "${bar:0:$menuwidth}"

  menunum=1

  ## loop through the positional parameters
  for item
  do
    var=${item%%:*}            ## variable name
    description=${item#*:}    ## variable description

    ## print item number, description and value
    printf "   %${#max}d: %s (%s)$clearEOL\n" \
             "$menunum" "$description" "${!var}"

    menunum=$(( $menunum + 1 ))
  done

  ## ... and menu adds its own items
  printf "   %${##}s\n" "q: Quit menu, start uploading" \
                  "0: Exit $scriptname"

  printf "\n${bar:0:$menuwidth}\n"    ## closing bar

  printf "$clearEOS\n" ## Clear to end of screen
  ##
  #########################################################

  #########################################################
  ## User selection and parameter input
  ##

  read -p " Select 1..$max or 'q' " $readopt x
  echo
```

```
    [ "$x" = q ] && break   ## User selected Quit
    [ "$x" = 0 ] && exit    ## User selected Exit

    case $x in
      *[!0-9]* | "")
              ## contains non digit or is empty
              printf "\a %s - Invalid entry\n" "$x" >&2
              sleep "$sleepytime"
              ;;
      *) if [ $x -gt $max ]
         then
           printf "\a %s - Invalid entry\n" "$x" >&2
           sleep "$sleepytime"
           continue
         fi

         var=${!x%%:*}
         description=${!x#*:}

         ## prompt user for new value
         printf "      %s$clearEOL\n" "$description"
         readline value "         >> "  "${!var}"

         ## if user did not enter anything, keep old value
         if [ -n "$value" ]
         then
           eval "$var=\$value"
         else
           printf "\a Not changed\n" >&2
           sleep "$sleepytime"
         fi
         ;;
    esac
    ##
    ############################################################

  done
}
```

Function: qa

The qa function takes the same arguments as menu, but instead of putting them into a menu, it prompts the user for a new value for each variable (Listing 12-10e). When it has run through all the command-line arguments, which it splits up in the same manner as menu, it calls the menu function for verification and editing of the values. Also like menu, it uses readline to get the input and keeps the old value if nothing is entered.

Listing 12-10e. Define qa Function

```
qa() #@ Question and answer dialog for variable entry
{
  local item var description

  printf "\n %s - %s\n" "$scriptname" "$description"
  printf " by %s, copyright %d\n" "$author" "$copyright"
  echo
  if [ ${BASH_VERSINFO[0]} -ge 4 ]
  then
    printf " %s\n" "You may edit existing value using the arrow keys."
  else
    printf " %s\n" "Press the up arrow to bring existing value" \
                   "to the cursor for editing with the arrow keys"
  fi
  echo

  for item
  do
    ## split $item into variable name and description
    var=${item%%:*}
    description=${item#*:}
    printf "\n %s\n" "$description"
    readline value "   >> " "${!var}"
    [ -n "$value" ] && eval "$var=\$value"
  done

  menu "$@"
}
```

The dialogue looks like this:

```
$ upload -qt

upload - Archive new or modified files and upload to web site
by Chris F.A. Johnson, copyright 2009

You may edit existing value using the arrow keys.


Remote host (URL or IP address)
  >> cfajohnson.com

SSH port
  >> 99

Destination directory
  >> public_html
```

```
Login name on remote system
  >> chris

Local directory to upload
  >> /home/chris/public_html/cfajonson.com

Directory to store archive files
  >> /home/chris/work/webarchives

File to touch with time of last upload
  >> .sync
```

Function: print_config

The print_config function prints all the variables listed in the varinfo array to the standard output in a format suitable for a configuration file, as described earlier in this chapter. Although probably not necessary in this program, it encloses the assignment value in double quotes and escapes double quotes in the value using bash's search-and-replace parameter expansion:

```
$ var=location
$ val='some"where'
$ printf "%s\n" "$var=\"${val//\"/\\\"}\""
location="some\"where"
```

See the options-parsing section in Listing 12-10f for an example of the output of print_config.

Listing 12-10f. Define print_config Function

```
print_config() #@ Print values in a format suitable for a configuration file
{
  local item var description

  [ -t 1 ] && echo  ## print blank line if output is to a terminal

  for item in "${varinfo[@]}"
  do
    var=${item%%:*}
    description=${item#*:}
    printf "%-35s ## %s\n" "$var=\"\${!var//\"/\\\"}\"" "$description"
  done

  [ -t 1 ] && echo  ## print blank line if output is to a terminal
}
```

Function: readline

If you are using bash-4.0 or later, the readline function will place a value before the cursor for you to edit (Listing 12-10g). With an earlier version of bash, it puts the value into the history so that you can bring it up with the up arrow (or Ctrl+P) and then edit it.

Listing 12-10g. Define readline Function

```
readline() #@ get line from user with editing of current value
{          #@ USAGE var [prompt] [default]
  local var=${1?} prompt=${2:-  >>> } default=$3

  if [ ${BASH_VERSINFO[0]} -ge 4 ]
  then
    read -ep "$prompt" ${default:+-i "$default"} "$var"
  else
    history -s "$default"
    read -ep "$prompt" "$var"
  fi
}
```

Parse Command-Line Options

You can set the seven configuration variables with the a, d, f, h, p, s, and u options. In addition, you can specify a configuration file with the c option. A test run, which prints the configuration information but doesn't attempt to create a tarball or upload any files, can be triggered with the t option. The m and q options offer the user a menu and a question-and-answer dialogue, respectively.

If a host is given as an option, a config file name is built using a standard formula. If the file exists, it is assigned to the configfile variable so that the parameters will be loaded from it. This is all usually I need to put on the command line (Listing 12-10h).

Listing 12-10h. Parse Command-Line Options

```
while getopts c:h:p:d:u:a:s:f:mqt var
do
  case "$var" in
    c) configfile=$OPTARG ;;
    h) host=$OPTARG
       hostconfig=$configdir/$scriptname.$host.cfg
       [ -f "$hostconfig" ] &&
         configfile=$hostconfig
       ;;
    p) port=$OPTARG ;;
    s) source=$OPTARG ;;
    d) dest=$OPTARG ;;
    u) user=$OPTARG ;;
    a) archivedir=$OPTARG ;;
    f) syncfile=$OPTARG ;;

    t) test=1 ;; ## show configuration, but do not archive or upload

    m) menu=1 ;;
    q) qa=1 ;;
  esac
done
shift $(( $OPTIND - 1 ))
```

Using options and redirection, this program can create new configuration files. Here, parameters are given on the command line, and defaults are used for those not given.

```
$ upload -t -h www.example.com -p 666 -u paradigm -d public_html \
  -s $HOME/public_html/www.example.com > www.example.com.cfg
$ cat www.example.com.cfg
host="www.example.com"                ## Remote host (URL or IP address)
port="666"                            ## SSH port
dest="public_html"                    ## Destination directory
user="paradigm"                       ## Login name on remote system
source="/home/chris/public_html/www.example.com" ## Local directory to upload
archivedir="/home/chris/work/webarchives" ## Directory to store archive files
syncfile=".sync"                      ## File to touch with time of last upload
```

Bits and Pieces

Listing 12-10i shows the rest of the script.

Listing 12-10i. The Rest of the Script

```
## If a configuration file is defined, try to load it
if [ -n "$configfile" ]
then
  if [ -f "$configfile" ]
  then
    ## exit if problem with config file
    . "$configfile" || die 1 Configuration error
  else
    ## Exit if configuration file is not found.
    die 2 "Configuration file, $configfile, not found"
  fi
fi

## Execute menu or qa if defined
if [ $menu -eq 1 ]
then
  menu "${varinfo[@]}"
elif [ $qa -eq 1 ]
then
  qa "${varinfo[@]}"
fi

## Create datestamped filename for tarball
tarfile=$archivedir/$host.$(date +%Y-%m-%dT%H:%M:%S.tgz)

if [ $test -eq 0 ]
then
  cd "$source" || die 4
fi
```

```
## verbose must be set (or not) in the environment or on the command line
if [ ${verbose:-0} -gt 0 ]
then
  printf "\nArchiving and uploading new files in directory: %s\n\n" "$PWD"
  opt=v
else
  opt=
fi

## IFS=$'\n' # uncomment this line if you have spaces in filenames (shame on you!)

if [ ${test:-0} -eq 0 ]
then
  remote_command="cd \"$dest\" || exit;tar -xpzf -"

  ## Archive files newer than $syncfile
  tar cz${opt}f "$tarfile" $( find . -type f -newer "$syncfile") &&

    ## Execute tar on remote computer with input from $tarfile
    ssh -p "$port" -l "$user" "$host" "$remote_command" < "$tarfile" &&

      ## if ssh is successful
      touch "$syncfile"

else ## test mode
  print_config
fi
```

Summary

This chapter demonstrated seven methods of altering the runtime behavior of a script. If changes will be rare, variables defined in the script may be adequate. When that isn't enough, command-line options (parsed with getopts) are often enough.

You can use a menu or question-and-answer dialogue both for runtime configuration and for creating configuration files that can be sourced on demand. Using differently named files for the same script can save typing. In some cases, setting a variable in the shell's environment is enough.

Exercises

1. Add code to the upload script that checks that all variables have been set to legitimate values (for example, that port is an integer).

2. Write a usage or help function, and add it to the upload script.

3. Add an option to the upload script to save the configuration if it has been saved.

4. Write a script that creates a configuration file in the same form as words.cfg, prompting the user for the information to put in it.

CHAPTER 13

■ ■ ■

Data Processing

Data manipulation includes a wide range of actions, far more than can be adequately covered in a single chapter. However, most actions are just the application of techniques already covered in earlier chapters. Arrays are a basic data structure, and although the syntax was covered in Chapter 5 and they were used in `fifteen` in Chapter 11, I haven't examined their uses. Parameter expansion has been used in a number of chapters, but its application to parsing data structures has not been discussed.

In this chapter, I'll cover different ways of using strings and arrays, how to parse character-delimited records into its individual fields, and how to read a data file. There are two function libraries for manipulating two-dimensional grids, and there are functions for sorting and searching arrays.

A number of the scripts in this chapter require `bash-3.1` or later.

Arrays

Arrays are not included in the POSIX shell, but bash has had indexed arrays since version 2.0, and in version 4.0, associative arrays were added. Indexed arrays are assigned and referenced using integer subscripts; associative arrays use strings. There is no preset limit to the number of elements an array can contain; they are limited only by available memory.

Holes in an Indexed Array

If some elements of an indexed array are unset, the array is left with holes; it becomes a sparse array. It will then be impossible to traverse the array merely by incrementing an index. There are various ways of dealing with such an array. To demonstrate, I'll create an array and poke some holes in it:

```
array=( a b c d e f g h i j )
unset array[2] array[4] array[6] array[8]
```

The array now contains six elements instead of the original ten:

```
$ sa "${array[@]}"
:a:
:b:
:d:
:f:
:h:
:j:
```

One way to iterate through all the remaining elements is to expand them as arguments to for. In this method, there is no way of knowing what the subscript for each element is:

```
for i in "${array[@]}"
do
   : do something with each element, $i, here
done
```

With a packed array (one with no holes), the index can start at 0 and be incremented to get the next element. With a sparse (or any) array, the ${!array[@]} expansion lists the subscripts:

```
$ echo "${!array[@]}"
0 1 3 5 7 9
```

This expansion can be used as the argument to for:

```
for i in "${!array[@]}"
do
   : do something with ${array[$i]} here
done
```

That solution gives you no method of referring to the next element. You can save the previous element but not get the value of the next one. To do that, you could put the list of subscripts into an array and use its elements to reference the original array. It's much simpler to pack the array, removing the holes:

```
$ array=( "${array[@]}" )
$ echo "${!array[@]}"
0 1 2 3 4 5
```

Note that this will convert an associative array to an indexed array.

Using an Array for Sorting

Ordering data alphabetically (or numerically) is not usually a task for the shell. The sort command is a very flexible and efficient tool that can handle most sorting needs. There are, however, a couple of cases where sorting can best be done by the shell.

The most obvious is file name expansion, in which the result of expanding wildcards is always sorted alphabetically. This is useful, for example, when working with date-stamped files. If the datestamp uses the standard ISO format, YYYY-MM-DD, or a compressed version, YYYYMMDD, the files will automatically be sorted in date order. If you have files in the format log.YYYYMMDD, this loops through them in chronological order:

```
for file in log.*    ## loop through files in chronological order
do
   : do whatever
done
```

There is no need to use ls; the shell sorts the wildcard expansion.

With bash-4.0, another expansion is sorted alphabetically: associative arrays with single-character subscripts:

```
$ declare -A q
$ q[c]=1 q[d]=2 q[a]=4
$ sa "${q[@]}"
:4:
:1:
:2:
```

This led me to write a function that sorts the letters of a word; see Listing 13-1.

Listing 13-1. lettersort, Sort Letters in a Word Alphabetically

```
lettersort() #@ Sort letters in $1, store in $2
{
  local letter string
  declare -A letters
  string=${1:?}
  while [ -n "$string" ]
  do
    letter=${string:0:1}
    letters["$letter"]=${letters["$letter"]}$letter
    string=${string#?}
  done
  printf -v "${2:-_LETTERSORT}" "%s" "${letters[@]}"
}
```

What's the point, you ask? Take a look at these examples:

```
$ lettersort triangle; printf "%s\n" "$_LETTERSORT"
aegilnrt
$ lettersort integral; printf "%s\n" "$_LETTERSORT"
aegilnrt
```

When the letters are sorted, you can see that the two words contain the same letters. Therefore, they are anagrams of each other. Try it with altering, alerting, and relating.

Insertion Sort Function

If you really want to do your sorting in the shell, you can. The function in Listing 13-2 is slower than the external sort command when there are more than 15 to 20 elements (the exact numbers will vary depending on your computer, its load, and so on). It inserts each element into the correct position in an array and then prints the resulting array.

Listing 13-2. isort, Sort Command-Line Arguments

```
isort()
{
  local -a a
  a=( "$1" ) ## put first argument in array for initial comparison
  shift      ## remove first argument
  for e      ## for each of the remaining arguments...
  do
    if [ "$e" \< "${a[0]}" ]                   ## does it precede the first element?
    then
      a=( "$e" "${a[@]}" )                     ## if yes, put it first
    elif [ "$e" \> "${a[${#a[@]}-1]}" ]        ## if no, does it go at the end?
    then
      a=( "${a[@]}" "$e" )                     ## if yes, put it at the end
    else                                       ## otherwise,
      n=0
      while [ "${a[$n]}" \< "$e" ]             ## find where it goes
      do
        n=$(( $n + 1 ))
      done
      a=( "${a[@]:0:n}" "$e" "${a[@]:n}" )  ## and put it there
    fi
  done
  printf "%s\n" "${a[@]}"
}
```

To put Canada's ten provincial capitals in alphabetical order, you'd use this:

```
$ isort "St. John's" Halifax Fredericton Charlottetown "Quebec City" \
                Toronto Winnipeg Regina Edmonton Victoria
Charlottetown
Edmonton
Fredericton
Halifax
Quebec City
Regina
St. John's
Toronto
Victoria
Winnipeg
```

Searching an Array

As with the isort function, this function is designed for use with relatively small arrays. If the array contains more than a certain number of elements (50? 60? 70?), it is faster to pipe it through grep. The function in Listing 13-3 takes the name of an array and a search string as arguments and stores elements containing the search string in a new array, _asearch_elements.

Listing 13-3. asearch, Search Elements of an Array for a String

```
asearch() #@ Search for substring in array; results in array _asearch_elements
{          #@ USAGE: asearch arrayname string
  local arrayname=$1 substring=$2   array

  eval "array=( \"\${$arrayname[@]}\" )"

  case ${array[*]} in
    *"$substring"*) ;;  ## it's there; drop through
    *) return 1 ;;      ## not there; return error
  esac

  unset _asearch_elements
  for subscript in "${!array[@]}"
  do
    case ${array[$subscript]} in
      *"$substring"*)
               _asearch_elements+=( "${array[$subscript]}" )
               ;;
    esac
  done
}
```

To see the function in action, put the provincial capitals from the previous section into an array, and call asearch:

```
$ capitals=( "St. John's" Halifax Fredericton Charlottetown "Quebec City"
                       Toronto Winnipeg Regina Edmonton Victoria )
$ asearch captials Hal && printf "%s\n"  "${_asearch_elements[@]}"
Halifax
$ asearch captials ict && printf "%s\n"  "${_asearch_elements[@]}"
Fredericton
Victoria
```

Reading an Array into Memory

There are various ways of reading a file into an array with bash. The most obvious is also the slowest: a while read loop:

```
unset array
while read line
do
  array+=( "$line" )
done < "$kjv"          ## kjv is defined in Chapter 8
```

A faster method that is still portable uses the external command, cat:

```
IFS=$'\n'              ## split on newlines, so each line is a separate element
array=( $(cat "$kjv") )
```

In bash, cat is unnecessary:

```
array=( < "$kjv" )     ## IFS is still set to a newline
```

With bash-4.0, a new builtin command, mapfile, is even faster:

```
mapfile -t array < "$kjv"
```

The options to mapfile allow you to select the line at which to start reading (actually, it's the number of lines to skip before starting to read), the number of lines to read, and the index at which to start populating the array. If no array name is given, the variable MAPFILE is used.

The following are the seven options to mapfile:

- -n num: Reads no more than num lines

- -O index: Begins populating the array at element index

- -s num: Discards the first num lines

- -t: Removes the trailing newline from each line

- -u fd: Reads from input stream fd instead of the standard input

- -C callback: Evaluates the shell command callback every N lines, where N is set by the following

- -c N: Specifies the number of lines between each evaluation of callback; the default is 5000

With older versions of bash, I used sed to extract ranges of lines from a file; with bash-4.0, I use mapfile. Listing 13-4 installs a function that uses mapfile if the version of bash is 4 or greater but sed uses if not:

Listing 13-4. getlines, Store a Range of Lines from a File in an Array

```
if [ "${BASH_VERSINFO[0]}" -ge 4 ]
then
  getlines() #@ USAGE: getlines file start num arrayname
  {
    mapfile -t -s$(( $2 - 1 )) -n ${3:?} "$4" < "$1"
  }
else
  getlines() #@ USAGE: getlines file start num arrayname
  {
    local IFS=$'\n' getlinearray arrayname=${4:?}
    getlinearray=( $(sed -n "$2,$(( $2 - 1 + $3 )) p" "$1") )
    eval "$arrayname=( \"\${getlinearray[@]}\" )"
  }
fi
```

Process substitution and external utilities can be used with mapfile to extract portions of a file using different criteria:

```
mapfile -t exodus < <(grep ^Exodus: "$kjv")      ## store the book of Exodus
mapfile -t books < <(cut -d: -f1 "$kjv" | uniq) ## store names of all books in KJV
```

Two-Dimensional Grids

I often find myself dealing with two-dimensional grids. As a constructor of crossword puzzles, I need to convert a grid from a puzzle file to a format that my client publications can import into desktop publishing software. As a chess tutor, I need to convert chess positions into a format that I can use in worksheets for my students. In games such as tic-tac-toe, maxit, and fifteen (from Chapter 11), the game board is a grid.

The obvious structure to use is a two-dimensional array. Since bash has only one-dimensional arrays, a workaround is needed to simulate two dimensions. This can be done as an array, a string, an array of strings, or a "poor-man's" array (see Chapter 9).

For a chess diagram, an associative array could be used, with the squares identified using the standard algebraic notation (SAN) for squares, a1, b1 to g8, h8:

```
declare -A chessboard
chessboard["a1"]=R
chessboard["a2"]=P
: ... 60 squares skipped
chessboard["g8"]=r
chessboard["h8"]=b
```

A structure I've used on a few occasions is an array in which each element is a string representing a rank:

```
chessboard=(
  RNBQKBRN
  PPPPPPPP
  "        "
  "        "
  "        "
  "        "
  pppppppp
  rnbqkbnr
)
```

My preference, when using bash, is a simple indexed array:

```
chessboardarray=(
R N B Q K B R N
P P P P P P P P
"" "" "" "" "" "" "" ""
"" "" "" "" "" "" "" ""
"" "" "" "" "" "" "" ""
"" "" "" "" "" "" "" ""
p p p p p p p p
r n b q k b n r
)
```

Or, in a POSIX shell, it could be a single string:

```
chessboard="RNBQKBRNPPPPPPPP                    pppppppprnbqkbnr"
```

Here are two function libraries, one for dealing with grids in a single string, the other for grids stored in arrays.

Working with Single-String Grids

I have a function library, `stringgrid-funcs`, for dealing with two-dimensional grids stored in a single string. There is a function to initialize all elements of a grid to a given character and one to calculate the index in the string of a character based on the x and y coordinates. There's one to fetch the character in the string using x/y and one to place a character into the grid at x/y. Finally, there are functions to print a grid, starting either with the first row or with the last row. These functions only work with square grids.

Function: initgrid

Given the name of the grid (that is, the variable name), the size, and optionally the character with which to fill it, initgrid (Listing 13-5a) creates a grid with the parameters supplied. If no character is supplied, a space is used.

The length of the string is the square of the grid size. A string of that length is created using a width specification in printf, with the -v option to save it to a variable supplied as an argument. Pattern substitution then replaces the spaces with the requested string.

This and the other functions in this library use the ${var:?} expansion, which displays an error and exits the script if there is no value for the parameter. This is appropriate because it is a programming error, not a user error if a parameter is missing. Even if it's missing because the user failed to supply it, it is still a programming error; the script should have checked that a value had been entered.

Listing 13-5a. initgrid, Create a Grid and Fill It

```
initgrid() #@ Fill N x N grid with a character
{            #@ USAGE: initgrid gridname size [character]
  ## If a parameter is missing, it's a programming error, so exit
  local grid gridname=${1:?} char=${3:- } size
  export gridsize=${2:?}              ## set gridsize globally

  size=$(( $gridsize ** 2 ))         ## total number of characters in grid
  printf -v grid "%$size.${size}s" " "  ## print string of spaces to variable
  eval "$gridname=\${grid// /"$char"}"  ## replace spaces with desired character
}
```

A tic-tac-toe grid is a string of nine spaces. For something this simple, the initgrid function is hardly necessary, but it is a useful abstraction:

```
$ . stringgrid-funcs
$ initgrid ttt 3
$ sa "$ttt"        ## The sa script/function has been used in previous chapters
:          :
```

Function: gridindex

To convert x and y coordinates into the corresponding position in the grid string, subtract 1 from the row number, multiply it by the gridsize, and add the columns. Listing 13-5b, gridindex, is a simple formula that could be used inline when needed, but again the abstraction makes using string grids easier and localizes the formula so that if there *is* a change, it only needs fixing in one place.

Listing 13-5b. gridindex, Calculate Index from Row and Column

```
gridindex() #@ Store row/column's index into string in var or $_gridindex
{          #@ USAGE: gridindex row column [gridsize] [var]]
  local row=${1:?} col=${2:?}

  ## If gridsize argument is not given, take it from definition in calling script
  local gridsize=${3:-$gridsize}
  printf -v "${4:-_GRIDINDEX}" "%d" "$(( ($row - 1) * $gridsize + $col - 1))"
}
```

What's the index of row 2, column 3 in the tic-tac-toe grid string?

```
$ gridindex 2 3    ## gridsize=3
$ echo "$_GRIDINDEX"
5
```

Function: putgrid

To change a character in the grid string, putgrid (Listing 13-5c) takes four arguments: the name of the variable containing the string, the row and column coordinates, and the new character. It splits the string into the part before the character and the part after it using bash's substring parameter expansion. It then sandwiches the new character between the two parts and assigns the composite string to the gridname variable. (Compare this with the _overlay function in Chapter 7.)

Listing 13-5c. putgrid, Insert Character in Grid at Specified Row and Column

```
putgrid() #@ Insert character int grid at row and column
{          #@ USAGE: putgrid gridname row column char
  local gridname=$1          ## grid variable name
  local left right           ## string to left and right of character to be changed
  local index                ## result from gridindex function
  local char=${4:?}          ## character to place in grid
  local grid=${!gridname}    ## get grid string though indirection

  gridindex ${2:?} ${3:?} "$gridsize" index

  left=${grid:0:index}
  right=${grid:index+1}
  grid=$left$4$right
  eval "$gridname=\$grid"
}
```

Here's the first move in a tic-tac-toe game:

```
$ putgrid ttt 1 2 X
$ sa "$ttt"
: X       :
```

Function: getgrid

The opposite of putgrid is getgrid (Listing 13-5d). It returns the character in a given position. Its arguments are the grid name (I could have used the string itself, because nothing is being assigned to it, but the grid name is used for consistency), the coordinates, and the name of the variable in which to store the character. If no variable name is supplied, it is stored in _GRIDINDEX.

Listing 13-5d. getgrid, Get Character at Row and Column Location in Grid

```
getgrid() #@ Get character from grid in row Y, column X
{          #@ USAGE: getgrid gridname row column var
  : ${1:?} ${2:?} ${3:?} ${4:?}
  local grid=${!1}
  gridindex "$2" "$3"
  eval "$4=\${grid:_GRIDINDEX:1}"
}
```

This snippet returns the piece in the square e1. A chess utility would convert the square to coordinates and then call the getgrid function. Here it is used directly.

```
$ gridsize=8
$ chessboard="RNBQKBRNPPPPPPPP                              pppppppprnbqkbnr"
$ getgrid chessboard 1 5 e1
$ sa "$e1"
:K:
```

Function: showgrid

This function (Listing 13-5e) extracts rows from a string grid using substring expansion and the gridsize variable and prints them to the standard output.

Listing 13-5e. showgrid, Print a Grid from a String

```
showgrid() #@ print grid in rows to stdout
{          #@ USAGE: showgrid gridname [gridsize]
  local grid=${!1:?} gridsize=${2:-$gridsize}
  local row     ## the row to be printed, then removed from local copy of grid

  while [ -n "$grid" ]  ## loop until there's nothing left
  do
    row=${grid:0:"$gridsize"}     ## get first $gridsize characters from grid
    printf "\t:%s:\n" "$row"      ## print the row
    grid=${grid#"$row"}           ## remove $row from front of grid
  done
}
```

Here we add another move to the tic-tac-toe board and display it:

```
$ gridsize=3     ## reset gridsize after changing it for the chessboard
$ putgrid ttt 2 2 O ## add O's move in the center square
$ showgrid ttt  ## print it
      : X :
      : O :
      :   :
```

Function: rshowgrid

For most grids, counting begins in the top-left corner. For others, such as a chessboard, it starts in the lower-left corner. To display a chessboard, the rgridshow function extracts and displays rows starting from the end of the string rather than from the beginning.

In Listing 13-5f, substring expansion is used with a negative.

Listing 13-5f. rshowgrid, Print a Grid in Reverse Order

```
rshowgrid() #@ print grid to stdout in reverse order
{            #@ USAGE: rshowgrid grid [gridsize]
  local grid gridsize=${2:-$gridsize} row
  grid=${!1:?}
  while [ -n "$grid" ]
  do
    ## Note space before minus sign
    ## to distinguish it from default value substitution
    row=${grid: -$gridsize}   ## get last row from grid
    printf "\t:%s:\n" "$row"  ## print it
    grid=${grid%"$row"}       ## remove it
  done
}
```

Here, rshowgrid is used to display the first move of a chess game. (For those who are interested, the opening is called Bird's Opening. It's not often played, but I have been using it successfully for 45 years.)

```
$ gridsize=8
$ chessboard="RNBQKBRNPPPPPPPP                                pppppppprnbqkbnr"
$ putgrid chessboard 2 6 ' '
$ putgrid chessboard 4 6 P
$ rshowgrid chessboard
      :rnbqkbnr:
      :pppppppp:
      :        :
      :        :
      :    P   :
      :        :
      :PPPPP PP:
      :RNBQKBRN:
```

These output functions can be augmented by piping the output through a utility such as sed or awk or even replaced with a custom function for specific uses. I find that the chessboard looks better when piped through sed to add some spacing:

```
$ rshowgrid chessboard | sed 's/./& /g' ## add a space after every character
        : r n b q k b n r :
        : p p p p p p p p :
        :                 :
        :                 :
        :         P       :
        :                 :
        : P P P P   P P :
        : R N B Q K B R N :
```

Two-Dimensional Grids Using Arrays

For many grids, a single string is more than adequate (and is portable to other shells), but an array-based grid offers more flexibility. In the fifteen puzzle in Chapter 11, the board is stored in an array. It is printed with printf using a format string that can easily be changed to give it a different look. The tic-tac-toe grid in an array could be as follows:

```
$ ttt=( "" X "" "" O "" "" X "" )
```

And this is the format string:

```
$ fmt="
     |   |
  %1s | %1s | %1s
 ----+---+----
  %1s | %1s | %1s
 ----+---+----
  %1s | %1s | %1s
     |   |

"
```

And the result, when printed, looks like this:

```
$ printf "$fmt" "${ttt[@]}"

     |   |
     | X |
 ----+---+----
     | O |
 ----+---+----
     | X |
     |   |
```

(This is an unusual position in that 0 will win no matter where he places his next 0.)

If the format string is changed to this:

```
fmt="

      _/      _/
   %1s  _/  %1s  _/  %1s
      _/      _/
_/_/_/_/_/_/_/_/_/
      _/      _/
   %1s  _/  %1s  _/  %1s
      _/      _/
_/_/_/_/_/_/_/_/_/
      _/      _/
   %1s  _/  %1s  _/  %1s
      _/      _/

"
```

the output will look like this:

```
   _/      _/
  _/  X  _/
   _/      _/
_/_/_/_/_/_/_/_/_/
   _/      _/
  _/  0  _/
   _/      _/
_/_/_/_/_/_/_/_/_/
   _/      _/
  _/  X  _/
   _/      _/
```

The same output could be achieved with a single-string grid, but it would require looping over every character in the string. An array is a group of elements that can be addressed individually or all at once, depending on the need.

The functions in arraygrid-funcs mirror those in stringgrid-funcs. In fact, the gridindex function is identical to the one in stringgrid-funcs, so it's not repeated here. As with the sdtring grid functions, some of them expect the size of the grid to be available in a variable, agridsize.

Function: initagrid

Most of the functions for array grids are simpler than their single-string counterparts. A notable exception is initagrid (Listing 13-6a), which is longer and slower, due to the necessity of a loop instead of a simple assignment. The entire array may be specified as arguments, and any unused array elements will be initialized to an empty string.

Listing 13-6a. initagrid, Initialize a Grid Array

```
initagrid() #@ Fill N x N grid with supplied data (or placeholders if none)
{            #@ USAGE: initgrid gridname size [character ...]
   ## If a required parameter is missing, it's a programming error, so exit
```

```
    local grid gridname=${1:?} char=${3:- } size
    export agridsize=${2:?}                ## set agridsize globally

    size=$(( $agridsize * $agridsize )) ## total number of elements in grid

    shift 2         ## Remove first two arguments, gridname and agridsize
    grid=( "$@" )   ## What's left goes into the array

    while [ ${#grid[@]} -lt $size ]
    do
      grid+=( "" )
    done

    eval "$gridname=( \"\${grid[@]}\" )"
}
```

Function: putagrid

Changing a value in an array is a straightforward assignment. Unlike changing a character in a string, there is no need to tear it apart and put it back together. All that's needed is the index calculated from the coordinates. This function (Listing 13-6b) requires agridsize to be defined.

Listing 13-6b. putagrid, Replace a Grid Element

```
putagrid() #@ Replace character in grid at row and column
{          #@ USAGE: putagrid gridname row column char
  local left right pos grid gridname=$1
  local value=${4:?} index
  gridindex ${2:?} ${3:?} "$agridsize" index   ## calculate the index
  eval "$gridname[index]=\$value"              ## assign the value
}
```

Function: getagrid

Given the x and y coordinates, getagrid fetches the value at that position and stores it in a supplied variable (Listing 13-6c).

Listing 13-6c. getagrid, Extract an Entry from a Grid

```
getagrid() #@ Get entry from grid in row Y, column X
{          #@ USAGE: getagrid gridname row column var
  : ${1:?} ${2:?} ${3:?} ${4:?}
  local grid

  eval "grid=( \"\${$1[@]}\" )"
  gridindex "$2" "$3"
  eval "$4=\${grid[$_GRIDINDEX]}"
}
```

Function: showagrid

showagrid (Listing 13-6d) prints each row of an array grid on a separate line.

Listing 13-6d. showagrid, Description

```
showagrid() #@ print grid to stdout
{          #@ USAGE: showagrid gridname format [agridsize]
  local gridname=${1:?} grid
  local format=${2:?}
  local agridsize=${3:-${agridsize:?}} row

  eval "grid=( \"\${$1[@]}\" )"
  printf "$format" "${grid[@]}"
}
```

Function: rshowagrid

rshowagrid (Listing 13-6e) prints each row of an array grid on a separate line in reverse order.

Listing 13-6e. rshowagrid, Description

```
rshowagrid() #@ print grid to stdout in reverse order
{            #@ USAGE: rshowagrid gridname format [agridsize]
  local format=${2:?} temp grid
  local agridsize=${3:-$agridsize} row
  eval "grid=( \"\${$1[@]}\" )"
  while [ "${#grid[@]}" -gt 0 ]
  do
    ## Note space before minus sign
    ## to distinguish it from default value substitution
    printf "$format" "${grid[@]: -$agridsize}"
    grid=( "${grid[@]:0:${#grid[@]}-$agridsize}" )
  done
}
```

Data File Formats

Data files are used for many purposes and come in many different flavors. These flavors are divided into two main types: line oriented and block oriented. In line-oriented files, each line is a complete record, usually with fields separated by a certain character. In block-oriented files, each record can span many lines, and there may be more than one block in a file. In some formats, a record is more than one block (a chess game in PGN format, for example, is two blocks separated by a blank line).

The shell is not the best language for working with large files of data; it is better working with individual records. However, there are utilities such as sed and awk that can work efficiently with large files and extract records to pass to the shell. This section deals with processing single records.

Line-Based Records

Line-based records are those where each line in the file is a complete record. It will usually be divided into fields by a delimiting character, but sometimes the fields are defined by length: the first 20 characters are the names, the next 20 are the first line of the address, and so on.

When the files are large, the processing is usually done by an external utility such as sed or awk. Sometimes an external utility will be used to select a few records for the shell to process. This snippet searches the password file for users whose shell is bash and feeds the results to the shell to perform some (unspecified) checks:

```
grep 'bash$' /etc/passwd |
while read line
do
  : perform some checking here
done
```

DSV: Delimiter-Separated Values

Most single-line records will have fields delimited by a certain character. In /etc/passwd, the delimiter is a colon. In other files, the delimiter may be a tab, tilde, or, very commonly, a comma. For these records to be useful, they must be split into their separate fields.

When records are received on an input stream, the easiest way to split them is to change IFS and read each field into its own variable:

```
grep 'bash$' /etc/passwd |
while IFS=: read user passwd uid gid name homedir shell
do
  printf "%16s: %s\n" \
      User        "$user" \
      Password    "$passwd" \
      "User ID"   "$uid" \
      "Group ID"  "$gid" \
      Name        "$name" \
"Home directory" "$homedir" \
      Shell       "$shell"

  read < /dev/tty
done
```

Sometimes it is not possible to split a record as it is read, such as if the record will be needed in its entirety as well as split into its constituent fields. In such cases, the entire line can be read into a single variable and then split later using any of several techniques. For all of these, we'll use the root entry from /etc/passwd:

```
record=root:x:0:0:root:/root:/bin/bash
```

The fields can be extracted one at a time using parameter expansion:

```
for var in user passwd uid gid name homedir shell
do
  eval "$var=\${record%%:*}"   ## extract the first field
  record=${record#*:}          ## and take it off the record
done
```

As long as the delimiting character is not found within any field, records can be split by setting IFS to the delimiter. When doing this, file name expansion should be turned off (with set -f) to avoid expanding any wildcard characters. The fields can be stored in an array and variables set to reference them:

```
IFS=:
set -f
data=( $record )
user=0
passwd=1
uid=2
gid=3
name=4
homedir=5
shell=6
```

The variable names are the names of the fields that can then be used to retrieve values from the data array:

```
$ echo;printf "%16s: %s\n" \
        User        "${data[$user]}" \
        Password    "${data[$passwd]}" \
        "User ID"   "${data[$uid]}" \
        "Group ID"  "${data[$gid]}" \
        Name        "${data[$name]}" \
"Home directory" "${data[$homedir]}" \
        Shell       "${data[$shell]}"

            User: root
        Password: x
         User ID: 0
        Group ID: 0
            Name: root
  Home directory: /root
           Shell: /bin/bash
```

It is more usual to assign each field to a scalar variable. This function (Listing 13-7a) takes a passwd record and splits it on colons and assigns fields to the variables.

Listing 13-7a. split_passwd, Split a Record from /etc/passwd into Fields and Assign to Variables

```
split_passwd() #@ USAGE: split_passwd RECORD
{
  local opts=$-     ## store current shell options
  local IFS=:
  local record=${1:?} array

  set -f                                 ## Turn off filename expansion
  array=( $record )                      ## Split record into array
  case $opts in *f*);; *) set +f;; esac  ## Turn on expansion if previously set
```

```
    user=${array[0]}
    passwd=${array[1]}
    uid=${array[2]}
    gid=${array[3]}
    name=${array[4]}
    homedir=${array[5]}
    shell=${array[6]}
}
```

The same thing can be accomplished using a *here document* (Listing 13-7b).

Listing 13-7b. split_passwd, Split a Record from /etc/passwd into Fields and Assign to Variables

```
split_passwd()
{
  IFS=: read user passwd uid gid name homedir shell <<.
$1
.
}
```

More generally, any character-delimited record can be split into variables for each field with this function (Listing 13-8).

Listing 13-8. split_record, Split a Record by Reading Variables

```
split_record() #@ USAGE parse_record record delimiter var ...
{
  local record=${1:?} IFS=${2:?} ## record and delimiter must be provided
  : ${3:?}                       ## at least one variable is required
  shift 2                        ## remove record and delimiter, leaving variables

  ## Read record into a list of variables using a 'here document'
  read "$@" <<.
$record
.
}
```

Using the record defined earlier, here's the output:

```
$ split_record "$record" : user passwd uid gid name homedir shell
$ sa "$user" "$passwd" "$uid" "$gid" "$name" "$homedir" "$shell"
:root:
:x:
:0:
:0:
```

```
:root:
:/root:
:/bin/bash:
```

Fixed-Length Fields

Less common than delimited fields are fixed-length fields. I don't use them often, but when I do, I loop through name=width strings to parse them:

```
line="John            123 Fourth Street   Toronto      Canada                      "
for nw in name=15 address=20 city=12 country=22
do
  var=${nw%%=*}                 ## variable name precedes the equals sign
  width=${nw#*=}                ## field width follows it
  eval "$var=\${line:0:width}"  ## extract field
  line=${line:width}           ## remove field from the record
done
```

Block File Formats

Among the many types of block data files I work with is the portable game notation (PGN) chess file. It stores one or more chess games in a format that is both human readable and machine readable. All chess programs can read and write this format.

Each game begins with a seven-tag roster that identifies where and when the game was played, who played it, and the result. This is followed by a blank line and then the moves of the game.

Here's a PGN chess game file, http://cfaj.freeshell.org/Fidel.pgn:

```
[Event "ICS rated blitz match"]
[Site "69.36.243.188"]
[Date "2009.06.07"]
[Round "-"]
[White "torchess"]
[Black "FidelCastro"]
[Result "1-0"]

1. f4 c5 2. e3 Nc6 3. Bb5 Qc7 4. Nf3 d6 5. b3 a6 6. Bxc6+ Qxc6 7. Bb2 Nf6
8. O-O e6 9. Qe1 Be7 10. d3 O-O 11. Nbd2 b5 12. Qg3 Kh8 13. Ne4 Nxe4 14.
Qxg7#
{FidelCastro checkmated} 1-0
```

I use a while loop to read the tags and then mapfile to get the moves of the game. The gettag function extracts the value from each tag and assigns it to the tag name (Listing 13-9).

Listing 13-9. readpgn, Parse a PGN Game and Print Game in a Column

```
pgnfile="${1:?}"
header=0
game=0
```

```
gettag() #@ create a variable with the same name and value as the tag
{
  local tagline=$1
  tag=${tagline%% *}        ## get line before the first space
  tag=${tag#?}              ## remove the open bracket
  IFS='"' read a val b <<.  ## get the 2nd field, using " as delimiter
   $tagline
.

  eval "$tag=\$val"
}

{
  while IFS= read -r line
  do
    case $line in
      \[*) gettag "$line" ;;
      "") [ -n "$Event" ] && break;;  ## skip blank lines at beginning of file
    esac
  done
  mapfile -t game                       ## read remainder of the file
} < "$pgnfile"

## remove blank lines from end of array
while [ -z "${game[${#game[@]}-1]}" ]
do
  unset game[${#game[@]}-1]
done

## print the game with header
echo "Event: $Event"
echo "Date:  $Date"
echo
set -f
printf "%4s  %-10s %-10s\n" "" White Black   "" ========== ========== \
         "" "$White" "$Black" ${game[@]:0:${#game[@]}-1}
printf "%s\n" "${game[${#game[@]}-1]}"
```

Summary

This chapter only scratched the surface of the possibilities for data manipulation, but I hope it will provide techniques to solve some of your needs and provide hints for others. Much of the chapter involved using that most basic of programming structures, arrays. Techniques were shown for working with single-line, character-delimited records, and basic techniques for working with blocks of data in files concluded the chapter.

Exercises

1. Modify the `isort` and `asearch` functions to use `sort` and `grep`, respectively, if the array exceeds a certain size.

2. Write a function that transposes rows and columns in a grid (either a single-string grid or an array). For example, transform this:

    ```
    123
    456
    789
    ```

    into this:

    ```
    147
    256
    369
    ```

3. Convert some of the grid functions, either string or array versions, to work with grids that are not square, for example, 6×3.

4. Convert the code that parses fixed-width records into a function that accepts the line of data as the first argument, followed by the `varname=width` list.

CHAPTER 14

■ ■ ■

Scripting the Screen

Unix purists will shake their heads over this chapter. Traditionally, screen manipulation is done through the `termcap` or `terminfo` database that supplies the information necessary to manipulate any of dozens or even hundreds of types of terminals. The shell interface to the database is an external command, `tput`.

On some systems, `tput` uses the `termcap` database; on others (mostly newer systems), it uses the `terminfo` database. The commands for the two databases are not the same, so a `tput` command written for one system may not work on another.

On one system, the command to place the cursor at the 20th column on the 10th row is as follows:

```
tput cup 9 19
```

On another system, this is the command:

```
tput cm 19 9
```

These commands will produce the correct output for whatever type of terminal is specified in the TERM variable. (Note: tput starts counting at 0.)

However, the plethora of terminal types has, for all intents and purposes, been reduced to a single, standard type. This standard, ISO 6429 (also known as ECMA-48 and formerly known as ANSI X3.64 or VT100), is ubiquitous, and terminals that do not support it are few and far between. As a result, it is now feasible to code for a single terminal type. One advantage of this homogeneity is that the necessary coding can be done entirely within the shell. There's no need for an external command.

Teletypewriter vs. Canvas

There are two methods of sending the output of a script to a terminal screen. The first and more traditional method uses the terminal as if it were a printer or teletypewriter (which is the origin of the abbreviation tty for the screen or terminal). In this mode, as each line is printed, the paper (or screen image) is scrolled up. Old lines fall to the floor (or disappear off the top of the screen). It's simple, and it is more than adequate for many applications.

The second method treats the screen as a blackboard or canvas and prints to specific points on its surface. It erases and overprints previously written sections. It may print text in columns or at specific locations on the screen. The terminal becomes a random-access, rather than serial, device.

This chapter is about the screen as canvas or blackboard. It defines a number of variables and functions for screen manipulation, as well as presenting some demonstration programs that use them.

Stretching the Canvas

To use the screen as a canvas, the most important capability is to be able to position the cursor at any given location on the screen. The sequence for that is ESC[<ROW>;<COL>H. When converted to a printf format string, it can be used directly or in a function.

```
cu_row_col=$'\e[%d;%dH'
printf "$cu_row_col" 5 10   ## Row 5, column 10
echo "Here I am!"
```

All the functions in this chapter are part of the screen-funcs library (Listing 14-1, sections *a* to *f*), which sources the screen-vars file (Listing 14-2, sections *a* to *d*).

Listing 14-1a. screen-funcs, Library of Screen Manipulation Functions

```
. screen-vars
```

The printat function (Listing 14-1b) places the cursor at the requested location and, if there are any further arguments, prints them. If the row and column are not specified, printat moves the cursor to the top-left corner of the screen.

Listing 14-1b. printat, Place the Cursor at a Specified Location and Print Optional String

```
printat() #@ USAGE: printat [row [column [string]]]
{
    printf "${cu_row_col?}" ${1:-1} ${2:-1}
    if [ $# -gt 2 ]
    then
      shift 2
      printf "%s" "$*"
    fi
}
```

CSI: Command Sequence Introducer

Like all the escape sequences, cu_row_col begins with ESC[. This is the command sequence introducer. I have it defined in my screen-vars file (Listing 14-2a).

Listing 14-2a. screen-vars, Screen Variable Definitions

```
ESC=$'\e'
CSI=$ESC[
```

Priming the Canvas

Before drawing on the screen, it must usually be cleared, and from time to time various parts of the screen will need to be cleared. These variables contain the fundamental sequences for clearing the screen or lines (Listing 14-2b).

Listing 14-2b. screen-vars, *Variable Definitions for Erasing All or Part of the Screen*

```
topleft=${CSI}H        ## move cursor to top left corner of screen
cls=${CSI}J            ## clear the screen
clear=$topleft$cls     ## clear the screen and move to top left corner
clearEOL=${CSI}K       ## clear from cursor to end of line
clearBOL=${CSI}1K      ## clear from cursor to beginning of line
clearEOS=${CSI}0J      ## clear from cursor to end of screen
clearBOS=${CSI}1J      ## clear from cursor to beginning of screen
```

Later in the chapter there are functions for clearing rectangular areas of the screen.

Moving the Cursor

Besides being moved to an absolute location, the cursor can be moved relative to its current position. The first four sequences are the same as those generated by the cursor keys, and they take arguments for moving more than one line or column. The next two turn the cursor on and off. The following two variables save the cursor position and move it back to the saved position, respectively.

The last two move to the next or previous line at the same column as the beginning of previously printed line. The printf specifier, %s, is removed because it would consume arguments that are to be printed (Listing 14-2c).

Listing 14-2c. screen-vars, *Variable Definitions for Moving the Cursor*

```
## cursor movement strings
     cu_up=${CSI}%sA
   cu_down=${CSI}%sB
  cu_right=${CSI}%sC
   cu_left=${CSI}%sD

## turn the cursor off and on
   cu_hide=${CSI}?25l
   cu_show=${CSI}?12l${CSI}?25h

## save the cursor position
   cu_save=${CSI}s              ## or ${ESC}7
## move cursor to saved position
cu_restore=${CSI}u             ## or ${ESC}8

## move cursor to next/previous line in block
     cu_NL=$cu_restore${cu_down/\%s/}$cu_save
     cu_PL=$cu_restore${cu_up/\%s/}$cu_save
```

The format strings for cursor movement use the %s specifier rather than %d, even though any argument will be a number. This is because printf replaces %d with a zero when there is no argument to fill it. If that happened, the cursor would not move at all. With %s, they move one column or row when there is no argument because %s is replaced by a null string.

The script in Listing 14-3 puts these variables and the printat function to work.

Listing 14-3. screen-demo1

```
. screen-funcs                              ## source the screen-funcs library
printf "$clear$cu_hide"                      ## Clear the screen and hide the cursor
printat 10 10 "${cu_save}XX"                 ## move, save position, and print XX
sleep 1                                      ## ZZZZZZZZ
printat 20 20 "20/20"                        ## move and print
sleep 1                                      ## ZZZZZZZZ
printf "$cu_restore$cu_down${cu_save}YY"      ## restore pos., move, print, save pos.
sleep 1                                      ## ZZZZZZZZ
printf "$cu_restore$cu_down${cu_save}ZZ" 4    ## restore pos., move, print, save pos.
sleep 1                                      ## ZZZZZZZZ
printat 1 1 "$cu_show"                        ## move to top left and show cursor
```

For a variation, try changing the coordinates of the first printat command to other values, say, 5 and 40.

Changing Rendition Modes and Colors

Characters can be printed in bold, underline, or reverse modes as well as in various colors for those terminals that support them (are there any left that don't?). These attributes are all modified with a sequence in the form ESC[ATTRm, where ATTR is the number of an attribute or color (Listing 14-2d). Multiple attributes can be specified by separating them with semicolons.

Colors are specified with integers 0 to 7 and 9 to reset to the default. These are prefixed by 3 for foreground color and 4 for background color. Attributes are also specified by 0 to 7 but without a prefix. Though eight attributes are defined, only three are widely supported: 1 (bold), 4 (underline), and 7 (reverse). These attributes can be turned off individually with the values 22, 24, and 27, respectively. A value of 0 resets all attributes and colors to their defaults.

Listing 14-2d. screen-vars, *Variable Definitions for Colors and Attributes*

```
## colours
  black=0
    red=1
  green=2
 yellow=3
   blue=4
magenta=5
   cyan=6
  white=7

    fg=3  ## foreground prefix
    bg=4  ## background prefix
```

```
## attributes
       bold=1
underline=4
  reverse=7

## set colors
    set_bg="${CSI}4%dm"           ## set background color
    set_fg="${CSI}3%dm"           ## set foreground color
  set_fgbg="${CSI}3%d;4%dm"       ## set foreground and background colors
```

As the next demonstration script shows, the colors and attributes can be used in "tty" mode as well as "canvas" mode (Listing 14-4).

Listing 14-4. screen-demo2

```
. screen-funcs
echo
for attr in "$underline" 0 "$reverse" "$bold" "$bold;$reverse"
do
  printf "$set_attr" "$attr"
  printf "$set_fg %s " "$red" RED
  printf "$set_fg %s " "$green" GREEN
  printf "$set_fg %s " "$blue" BLUE
  printf "$set_fg %s " "$black" BLACK
  printf "\e[m\n"
done
echo
```

Placing a Block of Text on the Screen

The put_block function prints its arguments one beneath the other at the current cursor position; put_block_at moves the cursor to the specified location, shifts the arguments to remove the row and column, and then calls put_block with the remaining arguments (Listing 14-1c).

The cu_NL variable moves the cursor to the saved position and then moves down a line and saves that position.

Listing 14-1c. put_block and put_block_at, Print a Block of Text Anywhere on the Screen

```
put_block() #@ Print arguments in a block beginning at the current position
{
  printf "$cu_save"        ## save cursor location
  printf "%s$cu_NL" "$@" ## restore cursor location, move line down, save cursor
}

put_block_at() #@ Print arguments in a block at the position in $1 and $2
{
  printat "$1" "$2"
  shift 2
  put_block "$@"
}
```

Listing 14-5 shows screen-demo3.

Listing 14-5. *screen-demo3*

```
. screenfuncs

printf "$cls"
put_block_at 3 12 First Second Third Fourth Fifth
put_block_at 2 50 January February March April May June July
```

The output of screen-demo3 is as follows:

```
                                          January
          First                           February
          Second                          March
          Third                           April
          Fourth                          May
          Fifth                           June
                                          July
```

The put_block and put_block_at functions work well when the screen is empty. If there's a lot of text already on the screen, the output may be obscured. For those cases, there are the print_block_at and print_block functions that clear a rectangular area around the block.

To determine the width that needs to be cleared, put_block passes its arguments to the _max_length function, which loops through the arguments to find the longest (Listing 14-1d).

Listing 14-1d. *_max_length, Store Length of Longest Argument in _MAX_LENGTH*

```
_max_length() #@ store length of longest argument in _MAX_LENGTH
{
  local var
  _MAX_LENGTH=${#1}       ## initialize with length of first parameter
  shift                   ## ...and remove first parameter
  for var                 ## loop through remaining parameters
  do
    [ "${#var}" -gt "$_MAX_LENGTH" ] && _MAX_LENGTH=${#var}
  done
}
```

The print_block function uses the result from _max_length as a width specification to printf (Listing 14-1e). Blank lines are printed before and after the text, and a space is printed before and after each line. The only difference between print_block_at and put_block_at is that one calls print_block and the other calls put_block.

Listing 14-1e. *print_block, Clear Area and Print Block*

```
print_block() #@ Print arguments in a block with space around them
{
  local _MAX_LENGTH
```

```
  _max_length "$@"
  printf "$cu_save"
  printf " %-${_MAX_LENGTH}s $cu_NL" " " "$@" " "
}

print_block_at() #@ Move to position, remove 2 parameters and call print_block
{
  printat $1 $2
  shift 2
  print_block "$@"
}
```

The text to be printed with either print_block or print_block is more likely to be a single string than separate arguments. To split up the string into words or phrases short enough to fit a given space, I use the wrap function (Listing 14-1f). This function splits a string into lines with a maximum width that is specified on the command line.

Listing 14-1f. wrap, Split String into Array with Elements Not Exceeding Maximum Length

```
wrap() #@ USAGE: wrap string length
{       #@ requires bash-3.1 or later
  local words=$1 textwidth=$2 line= opts=$-
  local len=0 templen=0
  set -f

  unset -v wrap
  for word in $words
  do
    templen=$(( $len + 1 + ${#word} )) ## Test adding a word
    if [ "$templen" -gt "$textwidth" ] ## Does adding a word exceed length?
    then
      wrap+=( "$line" )                ## Yes, store line in array
      printf -v line "%s" "$word"      ## begin new line
      len=${#word}
    else
      len=$templen                     ## No, add word to line
      printf -v line "%s" "${line:+"$line "}" "$word"
    fi
  done
  wrap+=( "$line" )

  case $opts in
    *f*) ;;
    *) set +f ;;
  esac
}
```

The sample shown in Listing 14-6 uses wrap and print_block_at.

Listing 14-6. `screen-demo4` *Demonstrates the* `wrap` *and* `print_block` *Functions*

```
clear
wrap "The quick brown fox jumps over the lazy dog" 15
x=xxxxxxxxxxxxxxxxxxxxxxxxxxxxxxxxxxxxxxxxxxxxxxxxxxxxxxxxxxxxxxxxxxxxxxxxxx
printat 1 1
printf "%s\n" $x{,,,,,,,,,,}          ## print 11 lines of 'x's
print_block_at 3 33 "${wrap[@]}"
printat 12 1
```

The output is as follows:

```
xxxxxxxxxxxxxxxxxxxxxxxxxxxxxxxxxxxxxxxxxxxxxxxxxxxxxxxxxxxxxxxxxxxxxxxxxx
xxxxxxxxxxxxxxxxxxxxxxxxxxxxxxxxxxxxxxxxxxxxxxxxxxxxxxxxxxxxxxxxxxxxxxxxxx
xxxxxxxxxxxxxxxxxxxxxxxxxxxxxxxxxx          xxxxxxxxxxxxxxxxxxxxxxxxxxxxxxxxxxxxx
xxxxxxxxxxxxxxxxxxxxxxxxxxxxxxxxxx The quick  xxxxxxxxxxxxxxxxxxxxxxxxxxxxxxxxxxxxx
xxxxxxxxxxxxxxxxxxxxxxxxxxxxxxxxxx brown fox jumps xxxxxxxxxxxxxxxxxxxxxxxxxxxxxxxx
xxxxxxxxxxxxxxxxxxxxxxxxxxxxxxxxxx over the lazy   xxxxxxxxxxxxxxxxxxxxxxxxxxxxxxxx
xxxxxxxxxxxxxxxxxxxxxxxxxxxxxxxxxx dog        xxxxxxxxxxxxxxxxxxxxxxxxxxxxxxxxxxxxx
xxxxxxxxxxxxxxxxxxxxxxxxxxxxxxxxx           xxxxxxxxxxxxxxxxxxxxxxxxxxxxxxxxxxxxx
xxxxxxxxxxxxxxxxxxxxxxxxxxxxxxxxxxxxxxxxxxxxxxxxxxxxxxxxxxxxxxxxxxxxxxxxxx
xxxxxxxxxxxxxxxxxxxxxxxxxxxxxxxxxxxxxxxxxxxxxxxxxxxxxxxxxxxxxxxxxxxxxxxxxx
xxxxxxxxxxxxxxxxxxxxxxxxxxxxxxxxxxxxxxxxxxxxxxxxxxxxxxxxxxxxxxxxxxxxxxxxxx
```

Scrolling Text

By combining an array with substring expansion, text can be scrolled in any area of the screen. Because the entire area can be printed with a single `printf` command, scrolling is fast, though it gets slower as the array size increases. The following demonstration (Listing 14-7) stores the file names in `/usr/bin/` in the array, `list`; scrolls the list up; waits for a second; and then scrolls it down.

Each loop, up and down, contains a commented-out `read -t "$delay"` line. When uncommented, it will slow down the scrolling. It uses the `bash-4.0` fractional delay. If you are using an earlier version, use `sleep` instead. Most implementations (certainly GNU and *BSD) accept a fractional argument.

Listing 14-7. `scroll-demo` *Scrolls a Block of Text Up and Then Down*

```
list=( /usr/bin/* )         ## try it with other directories or lists
rows=9                      ## number of rows in scrolling area
delay=.01                   ## delay between scroll advance
width=-33.33                ## width spec: (no more than) 33 chars, flush left
x=XXXXXXXXXXXXXXXXXXXXXXXXXX ## bar of 'X's
x=$x$x$x$x                  ## longer bar

clear                       ## clear the screen
printf "%50.50s\n" $x{,,,,,,,,,,,,,}      ## print 14 lines of 'X's

n=0                         ## start display with first element
```

```
## scroll upwards until reaching the bottom
while [ $(( n += 1 )) -lt $(( ${#list[@]} - $rows )) ]
do
  printf "\e[3;1H"
  printf "\e[7C %${width}s\n" "${list[@]:n:rows}"
#  read -sn1 -t "$delay" && break
done
sleep 1

## scroll downwards until reaching the top
while [ $(( n -= 1 )) -ge 0 ]
do
  printf "\e[3;1H"
  printf "\e[7C %${width}s\n" "${list[@]:n:rows}"
#  read -sn1 -t "$delay" && break
done

printf "\e[15;1H"    ## finish with cursor well below scrolling area
```

Rolling Dice

Dice are used in many games and are simple to program if you are satisfied with printing just the number:

```
printf "%s\n" "$(( $RANDOM % 6 + 1 ))"
```

However, a respectable graphical rendition can be programmed surprisingly easily with the shell. To print a die, position the cursor at the desired location on the screen, set the foreground and background colors, and print the element from the array (Figure 14-1).

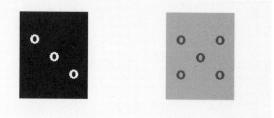

Figure 14-1. Listing 14-8 contains the code for these dice.

An array of six dice can be programmed in about 25 lines of code. Each die is a concatenation of 18 variables. Some of these have the same contents as those in the screen-funcs library, but their names are shortened here to keep the lines shorter. Here is a description of the die with the number 5:

```
$b    ## set bold attribute (optional)
$cs   ## save cursor position
$p0   ## print blank row
$cr   ## restore cursor to left side of die
$dn   ## move down one line
```

```
$cs    ## save cursor position
$p4    ## print row with two pips
$cr    ## restore cursor to left side of die
$dn    ## move down one line
$cs    ## save cursor position
$p2    ## print row with one pip
$cr    ## restore cursor to left side of die
$dn    ## move down one line
$cs    ## save cursor position
$p4    ## print row with two pips
$cr    ## restore cursor to left side of die
$dn    ## move down one line
$p0    ## print blank row
```

After defining the dice, the script in Listing 14-8 clears the screen and prints two random dice near the top of the screen.

Listing 14-8. dice Defines an Array of Six Dice and Places Two on the Screen

```
pip=o                        ## character to use for the pips
p0="          "              ## blank line
p1=" $pip     "              ## one pip at the left
p2="    $pip     "           ## one pipe in the middle of the line
p3="      $pip "             ## one pip at the right
p4=" $pip   $pip "           ## two pips
p5=" $pip $pip $pip "        ## three pips

cs=$'\e7'                    ## save cursor position
cr=$'\e8'                    ## restore cursor position
dn=$'\e[B'                   ## move down 1 line
b=$'\e[1m'                   ## set bold attribute
cu_put='\e[%d;%dH'           ## format string to position cursor
fgbg='\e[3%d;4%dm'           ## format string to set colors

dice=(
  ## dice with values 1 to 6 (array elements 0 to 5)
  "$b$cs$p0$cr$dn$cs$p0$cr$dn$cs$p2$cr$dn$cs$p0$cr$dn$p0"
  "$b$cs$p0$cr$dn$cs$p1$cr$dn$cs$p0$cr$dn$cs$p3$cr$dn$p0"
  "$b$cs$p0$cr$dn$cs$p1$cr$dn$cs$p2$cr$dn$cs$p3$cr$dn$p0"
  "$b$cs$p0$cr$dn$cs$p4$cr$dn$cs$p0$cr$dn$cs$p4$cr$dn$p0"
  "$b$cs$p0$cr$dn$cs$p4$cr$dn$cs$p2$cr$dn$cs$p4$cr$dn$p0"
  "$b$cs$p0$cr$dn$cs$p5$cr$dn$cs$p0$cr$dn$cs$p5$cr$dn$p0"
  )

clear
printf "$cu_put" 2 5         ## position cursor
printf "$fgbg" 7 0           ## white on black
printf "%s\n" "${dice[RANDOM%6]}"  ## print random die

printf "$cu_put" 2 20        ## position cursor
printf "$fgbg" 0 3           ## black on yellow
printf "%s\n" "${dice[RANDOM%6]}"  ## print random die
```

Summary

Without touching on traditional ASCII art, there are many ways to draw things on a terminal screen. This chapter has presented a number of them, giving the basics that can be used to create many more.

Exercises

1. Write a function, hbar, that accepts two integer arguments, a width and a color, and prints a bar of that color and width. Write a second function, hbar_at, that accepts four arguments, row, column, width and color; moves the cursor to the row and column; and passes the remaining arguments to hbar.

2. White a function, clear_area, that accepts two integer arguments, rows and columns, and clears a rectangular area of that many rows and columns.

CHAPTER 15

■■■

Entry-Level Programming

My preference for bash over any other POSIX shell stems to a great extent from its extensions that enhance interactive programming. The extended options to the read builtin command (which were described in Chapter 9), combined with the history and readline libraries, add functionality that no other shell can match.

Despite its richness, there is still no easy way for the shell to deal with keys such as function keys that generate multiple characters. For that, I present the key-funcs library of functions. The second major section of this chapter describes how to use the mouse in shell scripts and provides a demonstration program.

Between those sections, I deal with checking user input for validity and the history library. Most people use bash's history library only at the command line. I use it in scripts, and in this chapter I show how that is done. I demonstrate the history command in a rudimentary script for editing a multifield record.

Single-Key Entry

When writing an interactive script, I often want a single key to be pressed without requiring the user to press Enter. The portable way to do that is to use stty and dd:

```
stty -echo -icanon min 1
_KEY=$(dd count=1 bs=1 2>/dev/null)
stty echo icanon
```

I don't like using three external commands every time I need a keypress. When I need to use a portable method, I usually do the first call to stty at the beginning of the script and the other at the end, often in an EXIT trap:

```
trap 'stty echo icanon' EXIT
```

Bash, on the other hand, doesn't need to call any external commands. It may still be a good idea to use stty to turn off echoing at the beginning and back on before exiting. This will prevent characters showing up on the screen when the script is not waiting for input.

Function Library, key-funcs

The functions in this section comprise the key-funcs library. It begins with two variable definitions, shown here in Listing 15-1.

Listing 15-1. key-funcs, Read a Single Keypress

```
ESC=$'\e'
CSI=$'\e['
```

To get a single keystroke with bash, I can use the function in Listing 15-1a.

Listing 15-1a. _key, Functions for Reading a Single Keypress

```
_key()
{
    IFS= read -r -s -n1 -d '' "${1:-_KEY}"
}
```

First, the field separator is set to an empty string so that read doesn't ignore a leading space (it's a valid keystroke, so you want it); the -r option disables backslash escaping, -s turns off echoing of keystrokes, and -n1 tells bash to read a single character only.

The -d '' option tells read not to regard a newline (or any other character) as the end of input; this allows a newline to be stored in a variable. I have told read to stop after the first key is received (-n1) so it doesn't read forever.

The last argument uses ${@:-_KEY} to add options and/or a variable name to the list of arguments. You can see its use in the _keys function in Listing 15-2. (Note that if you use an option without also including a variable name, the input will be stored in $REPLY.)

The _key function can be used in a simple menu, as shown in Listing 15-2.

Listing 15-2. simplemenu, a Menu That Responds to a Single Keypress

```
## the _key function should be defined here if it is not already
while :
do
  printf "\n\n\t$bar\n"
  printf "\t %d. %s\n" 1 "Do something" \
                       2 "Do something else" \
                       3 "Quit"
  printf "\t%s\n" "$bar"
  _key
  case $_KEY in
     1) printf "\n%s\n\n" Something ;;
     2) printf "\n%s\n\n" "Something else" ;;
     3) break ;;
     *) printf "\a\n%s\n\n" "Invalid choice; try again"
        continue
        ;;
  esac
  printf ">>> %s " "Press any key to continue"
  _key
done
```

Although _key is a useful function by itself, it has its limitations (Listing 15-1b). It can store a space, a newline, a control code, or any other single character, but what it doesn't do is handle keys that return more than one character: function keys, cursor keys, and a few others.

These special keys return ESC (0x1B, which I keep in a variable $ESC) followed by one or more characters. The number of characters varies according to the key (and the terminal emulation), so you cannot ask for a specific number of keys. Instead, you have to loop until one of the terminating characters is read. This is where it helps to use bash's built-in read command rather than the external dd.

Listing 15-1b. _keys, Read a Sequence of Characters from a Function or Cursor Key

```
_keys() #@ Store all waiting keypresses in $_KEYS
{
    _KEYS=
    __KX=

    ## ESC_END is a list of characters that can end a key sequence
    ## Some terminal emulations may have others; adjust to taste
    ESC_END=[a-zA-NP-Z~^\$@$ESC]

    while :
    do
      IFS= read -rsn1 -d '' -t1 __KX
      _KEYS=$_KEYS$__KX
      case $__KX in
            "" | $ESC_END ) break ;;
      esac
    done
}
```

The while : loop calls _key with the argument -t1, which tells read to time out after one second, and the name of the variable in which to store the keystroke. The loop continues until a key in $ESC_END is pressed or read times out, leaving $__KX empty.

The timeout is a partially satisfactory method of detecting the escape key by itself. This is a case where dd works better than read, because it can be set to time out in increments of one tenth of a second.

To test the functions, I use _key to get a single character; if that character is ESC, I call _keys to read the rest of the sequence, if any. The following snippet assumes that _key and _keys are already defined and pipes each keystroke through hexdump -C to show its contents:

```
while :
do
  _key
  case $_KEY in
      $ESC) _keys
            _KEY=$ESC$_KEYS
            ;;
  esac
  printf "%s" "$_KEY" | hexdump -C | {
                read a b
                printf "    %s\n" "$b"
            }
  case "$_KEY" in q) break ;; esac
done
```

Unlike the output sequences, which work everywhere, there is no homogeneity among key sequences produced by various terminal emulators. Here is a sample run, in an rxvt terminal window, of pressing F1, F12, up arrow, Home, and q to quit:

```
1b 5b 31 31 7e        |.[11~|
1b 5b 32 34 7e        |.[24~|
1b 5b 41              |.[A|
1b 5b 35 7e           |.[5~|
71                    |q|
```

Here are the same keystrokes in an xterm window:

```
1b 4f 50              |.OP|
1b 5b 32 34 7e        |.[24~|
1b 5b 41              |.[A|
1b 5b 48              |.[H|
71                    |q|
```

Finally, here they are as produced by a Linux virtual console:

```
1b 5b 5b 41           |.[[A|
1b 5b 32 34 7e        |.[24~|
1b 5b 41              |.[A|
1b 5b 31 7e           |.[1~|
71                    |q|
```

All the terminals I've tested fit into one of these three groups, at least for unmodified keys.

The codes stored in $_KEY can be either interpreted directly or in a separate function. I like to keep the interpretation in a function that can be replaced for use with different terminal types. For example, if I am using a Wyse60 terminal, I could source wy60-keys for a replacement function.

Listing 15-1c shows a function, _esc2key, that works for the various terminals on my Linux box, as well as in putty in Windows. It converts the character sequence into a string describing the key, for example, UP, DOWN, F1 and so on:

Listing 15-1c. _esc2key, *Translate a String to a Key Name*

```
_esc2key()
{
  case $1 in
    ## Cursor keys
    "$CSI"A | ${CSI}OA ) _ESC2KEY=UP ;;
    "$CSI"B | ${CSI}OB ) _ESC2KEY=DOWN ;;
    "$CSI"C | ${CSI}OC ) _ESC2KEY=RIGHT ;;
    "$CSI"D | ${CSI}OD ) _ESC2KEY=LEFT ;;

    ## Function keys (unshifted)
    "$CSI"11~ | "$CSI["A | ${ESC}OP ) _ESC2KEY=F1 ;;
    "$CSI"12~ | "$CSI["B | ${ESC}OQ ) _ESC2KEY=F2 ;;
    "$CSI"13~ | "$CSI["C | ${ESC}OR ) _ESC2KEY=F3 ;;
    "$CSI"14~ | "$CSI["D | ${ESC}OS ) _ESC2KEY=F4 ;;
```

```
    "$CSI"15~ | "$CSI["E ) _ESC2KEY=F5 ;;
    "$CSI"17~ | "$CSI["F ) _ESC2KEY=F6 ;;
    "$CSI"18~ ) _ESC2KEY=F7 ;;
    "$CSI"19~ ) _ESC2KEY=F8 ;;
    "$CSI"20~ ) _ESC2KEY=F9 ;;
    "$CSI"21~ ) _ESC2KEY=F10 ;;
    "$CSI"23~ ) _ESC2KEY=F11 ;;
    "$CSI"24~ ) _ESC2KEY=F12 ;;

    ## Insert, Delete, Home, End, Page Up, Page Down
    "$CSI"2~ ) _ESC2KEY=INS ;;
    "$CSI"3~ ) _ESC2KEY=DEL ;;
    "$CSI"[17]~ | "$CSI"H ) _ESC2KEY=HOME ;;
    "$CSI"[28]~ | "$CSI"F ) _ESC2KEY=END ;;
    "$CSI"5~ ) _ESC2KEY=PGUP ;;
    "$CSI"6~ ) _ESC2KEY=PGDN ;;

    ## Everything else; add other keys before this line
    *) _ESC2KEY=UNKNOWN ;;
  esac
  [ -n "$2" ] && eval "$2=\$_ESC2KEY"
}
```

I wrap the _key and _esc2key functions in another function, called get_key (Listing 15-1d), which returns either the single character pressed or, in the case of multicharacter keys, the name of the key:

Listing 15-1d. get_key, Gets a Key and, If Necessary, Translates It to a Key Name

```
get_key()
{
    _key
    case $_KEY in
        "$ESC") _keys
                _esc2key "$ESC$_KEYS" _KEY
                ;;
    esac
}
```

In bash-4.0, I use a simpler function to read keystrokes. The get_key function in Listing 15-1e takes advantage of the capability of read's -t option to accept fractional times. It reads the first character then waits for one ten-thousandth of a second for another character. If a multicharacter key was pressed, there will be one to read within that time. If not, it will fall through the remaining read statements before another key can be pressed.

Listing 15-1e. get_key, Reads a Key and, If It Is More Than a Single Character, Translates It to a Key Name

```
get_key() #@ USAGE: get_key var
{
    local _v_ _w_ _x_ _y_ _z_ delay=${delay:-.0001}
    IFS= read -d '' -rsn1 _v_
```

```
  read -sn1 -t "$delay" _w_
  read -sn1 -t "$delay" _x_
  read -sn1 -t "$delay" _y_
  read -sn1 -t "$delay" _z_
  case $_v_ in
    $'\e') _esc2key "$_v_$_w_$_x_$_y_$_z_"
           printf -v ${1:?} $_ESC2KEY
           ;;
    *) printf -v ${1:?} "%s" "$_v_$_w_$_x_$_y_$_z_" ;;
  esac
}
```

Whenever I want to use cursor or function keys in a script, or for any single-key entry, I source key-funcs and call get_key to capture keypresses. Listing 15-3 is a simple demonstration of using the library.

Listing 15-3. keycapture, Read and Display Keystrokes Until Q Is Pressed

```
. key-funcs                      ## source the library
while :                          ## infinite loop
do
  get_key key
  sa "$key"                      ## the sa command is from previous chapters
  case $key in q|Q) break;; esac
done
```

The script in Listing 15-4 prints a block of text on the screen. It can be moved around the screen with the cursor keys, and the colors can be changed with the function keys. The odd-numbered function keys change the foreground color; the even-numbered keys change the background.

Listing 15-4. key-demo, Capture Function and Cursor Keys to Change Colors and Move a Block of Text Around the Screen

```
trap '' 2
trap 'stty sane; printf "${CSI}?12l${CSI}?25h\e[0m\n\n"' EXIT

stty -echo   ## Turn off echoing of user keystrokes
. key-funcs  ## Source key functions

clear        ## Clear the screen
bar===================================

## Initial position for text block
row=$(( (${LINES:-24} - 10) / 2 ))
col=$(( (${COLUMNS:-80} - ${#bar}) / 2 ))

## Initial colours
fg="${CSI}33m"
bg="${CSI}44m"
```

```
## Turn off cursor
printf "%s" "${CSI}?25l"

## Loop until user presses "q"
while :
do
  printf "\e[1m\e[%d;%dH" "$row" "$col"
  printf "\e7 %-${#bar}.${#bar}s ${CSI}0m   \e8\e[1B" "${CSI}0m"
  printf "\e7 $fg$bg%-${#bar}.${#bar}s${CSI}0m \e8\e[1B" "$bar" \
              "" " Move text with cursor keys" \
              "" " Change colors with function keys" \
              "" " Press 'q' to quit" \
              "" "$bar"
  printf "\e7%-${#bar}.${#bar}s        " "${CSI}0m"
  get_key k
  case $k in
      UP) row=$(( $row - 1 )) ;;
      DOWN) row=$(( $row + 1 )) ;;
      LEFT) col=$(( $col - 1 )) ;;
      RIGHT) col=$(( $col + 1 )) ;;
      F1) fg="${CSI}30m" ;;
      F2) bg="${CSI}47m" ;;
      F3) fg="${CSI}31m" ;;
      F4) bg="${CSI}46m" ;;
      F5) fg="${CSI}32m" ;;
      F6) bg="${CSI}45m" ;;
      F7) fg="${CSI}33m" ;;
      F8) bg="${CSI}44m" ;;
      F9) fg="${CSI}35m" ;;
      F10) bg="${CSI}43m" ;;
      F11) fg="${CSI}34m" ;;
      F12) bg="${CSI}42m" ;;
      q|Q) break ;;
  esac
  colmax=$(( ${COLUMNS:-80} - ${#bar} - 4 ))
  rowmax=$(( ${LINES:-24} - 10 ))
  [ $col -lt 1 ] && col=1
  [ $col -gt $colmax ] && col=$colmax
  [ $row -lt 1 ] && row=1
  [ $row -gt $rowmax ] && row=$rowmax
done
```

History in Scripts

In the readline functions in Chapters 6 and 12, history -s was used to place a default value into the history list. In those examples, only one value was stored, but it is possible to store more than one value in history or even to use an entire file. Before adding to the history, you should (in most cases) clear it:

```
history -c
```

By using more than one `history -s` command, you can store multiple values:

```
history -s Genesis
history -s Exodus
```

With the `-r` option, you can read an entire file into history. This snippet puts the names of the first five books of the Bible into a file and reads that into the history:

```
cut -d: -f1 "$kjv" | uniq | head -5 > pentateuch
history -r pentateuch
```

The `readline` functions in Chapters 6 and 12 use `history` if the bash version is less than 4, but read's `-i` option with version 4 (or greater). There are times when it might be more appropriate to use `history` rather than `-i` even when the latter is available. A case in point is when the new input is likely to be very different from the default but there is a chance that it might not be.

For history to be available, you must use the `-e` option with read. This also gives you access to other key bindings defined in your `.inputrc` file.

Sanity Checking

Sanity checking is testing input for the correct type and a reasonable value. If a user inputs *Jane* for her age, it's obviously wrong: the data is of the wrong type. If she enters *666*, it's the correct type but almost certainly an incorrect value. The incorrect type can easily be detected with the `valint` script (Chapter 3) or function (Chapter 6). You can use the `rangecheck` function from Chapter 6 to check for a reasonable value.

Sometimes, the error is more problematic, or even malicious. Suppose a script asks for a variable name and then uses eval to assign a value to it:

```
read -ep "Enter variable name: " var
read -ep "Enter value: " val
eval "$var=\$val"
```

Now, suppose the entry goes like this:

```
Enter variable name: rm -rf *;name
Enter value: whatever
```

The command that eval will execute is as follows:

```
rm -rf *;name=whatever
```

Poof! All your files and subdirectories are gone from the current directory. It could have been prevented by checking the value of var with the `validname` function from Chapter 7:

```
validname "$var" && eval "$var=\$val" || echo Bad variable name >&2
```

When editing a database, checking that there are no invalid characters is an important step. For example, in editing /etc/passwd (or a table from which it is created), you must make sure that there are no colons in any of the fields.

Cartoon courtesy of Randall Munroe at http://xkcd.com.

Form Entry

The script in Listing 15-5 is a demonstration of handling user input with a menu and history. It uses the key-funcs library to get the user's selection and to edit password fields. It has a hard-coded record and doesn't read the /etc/passwd file. It checks for a colon in an entry and prints an error message if one is found.

The record is read into an array from a here document. A single printf statement prints the menu, using a format string with seven blanks and the entire array as its arguments.

Listing 15-5. password, a Simple Record-Editing Script

```
record=root:x:0:0:root:/root:/bin/bash          ## record to edit
fieldnames=( User Password UID
             GID Name Home Shell )

. key-funcs                                      ## load the key functions

IFS=: read -a user <<EOF                         ## read record into array
$record
```

```
EOF

z=0
clear
while :                                  ## loop until user presses 0 or q
do
  printf "\e[H\n
   0.      Quit
   1.     User: %s\e[K
   2. Password: %s\e[K
   3.      UID: %s\e[K
   4.      GID: %s\e[K
   5.     Name: %s\e[K
   6.     Home: %s\e[K
   7.    Shell: %s\e[K

    Select field (1-7): \e[0J" "${user[@]}"   ## print menu and prompt

  get_key field                          ## get user input

  printf "\n\n"                          ## print a blank line
  case $field in
   0|q|Q) break ;;                       ## quit
   [1-7]) ;;                             ## menu item selected; fall through
   *) continue;;
  esac
  history -c                             ## clear history
  history -s "${user[field-1]}"          ## insert current value in history
  printf '  Press UP to edit "%s"\n' "${user[field-1]}" ## tell user what's there
  read -ep "          ${fieldnames[field-1]}: " val      ## get user entry
  case $val in
    *:*) echo "     Field may not contain a colon (press ENTER)" >&2  ## ERROR
         get_key; continue
         ;;
    "") continue ;;
    *) user[field-1]=$val ;;
  esac
done
```

Reading the Mouse

While reading the Linux console_codes man page, I came across a section labeled "mouse tracking." Interesting! I read on: "The mouse tracking facility is intended to return xterm-compatible mouse status reports." Does that mean, I wondered, that I can use the mouse in shell scripts?

According to that man page, mouse tracking is available in two modes: X10 compatibility mode, which sends an escape sequence on button press, and normal tracking mode, which sends an escape sequence on both button press and release. Both modes also send modifier-key information.

To test this, I went to a terminal window and entered printf "\e[?9h". I pressed the mouse button, and the computer beeped at me and printed " FB" on the screen. Repeating the mouse click at various points on the screen netted me more beeps and " &% -(5. =2 H7 T=]C fG rJ }M."

A mouse click sends six characters: ESC, [, M, *b*, *x*, *y*. The first three characters are common to all mouse events, the second three contain the button pressed, and the finals ones are the *x* and *y* locations of the mouse. To confirm this, I saved the input in a variable and piped it to hexdump:

```
$ printf "\e[?9h"
$ read x
^[[M!MO                ## press mouse button and enter
$ printf "$x" | hexdump -C
00000000  1b 5b 4d 21 4d 4f                         |.[M!MO|
00000006
```

The first three appear as expected, but what are the final three? According to the man page, the lower two bits of the button character tell which button has been pressed; the upper bits identify the active modifiers. The *x* and *y* coordinates are the ASCII values to which 32 has been added to take them out of the range of control characters. ! is 1, " is 2, and so on.

That gives us a 1 for the mouse button (which means button 2, since 0 to 2 are buttons 1, 2, and 3, respectively, and 4 is release. The *x* and *y* coordinates are 45 (Ox4d=77; 77−32=45) and 47.

Surprisingly, since I read about mouse tracking in a Linux console_codes man page, these escape codes do not work in any Linux console that I have tried. They work in xterm, rxvt, and gnome-terminal on Linux and FreeBSD. I've used them on FreeBSD and NetBSD, via ssh from a Linux rxvt terminal window. They do not work in a KDE konsole window.

You now know that mouse reporting works (in most xterm windows), and you can get information from a mouse click on the standard input. That leaves two questions: how do you read the information into a variable (without having to press Return), and how can the button and *x*, *y* information be decoded in a shell script?

With bash, use the read command's -n option with an argument to specify the number of characters. To read the mouse, six characters are needed:

```
read -n6 x
```

Neither of these is adequate for a real script (not all input will be mouse clicks, and you will want to get single keystrokes), but they suffice to demonstrate the concept.

The next step is to decode the input. For the purpose of this demonstration, you can assume that the six characters do indeed represent a mouse click and that the first three characters are ESC, [, and M. I'm only interested in the last three, so I extract them into three separate variables using POSIX parameter expansion:

```
m1=${x#???}     ## Remove the first 3 characters
m2=${x#????}    ## Remove the first 4 characters
m3=${x#?????}   ## Remove the first 5 characters
```

Then I convert the first character of each variable to its ASCII value. This uses a POSIX printf extension, "If the leading character is a single-quote or double-quote, the value shall be the numeric value in the underlying codeset of the character following the single-quote or double-quote."[1]

```
printf -v mb "%d" "'$m1"
printf -v mx "%d" "'$m2"
printf -v my "%d" "'$m3"
```

---

[1] http://www.opengroup.org/onlinepubs/9699919799/utilities/printf.html

Finally, I interpret the ASCII values. For the mouse button, I do a bitwise AND 3. For the *x* and *y* coordinates, I subtract 32:

```
## Values > 127 are signed, so fix if less than 0
[ $mx -lt 0 ] && mx=$(( 255 + $mx ))
[ $my -lt 0 ] && my=$(( 255 + $my ))

BUTTON=$(( ($mb & 3) + 1 ))
MOUSEX=$(( $mx - 32 ))
MOUSEY=$(( $my - 32 ))
```

Putting it all together, the script in Listing 15-6 prints the mouse's coordinates whenever you press a mouse button.

There are two sensitive areas on the top row. Clicking the left one toggles the mouse reporting mode between reporting only a button press and reporting the release as well. Clicking the right one exits the script.

Listing 15-6. *mouse-demo, an Example of Reading Mouse Clicks*

```
ESC=$'\e'
but_row=1

mv=9  ## mv=1000 for press and release reporting; mv=9 for press only

_STTY=$(stty -g)       ## Save current terminal setup
stty -echo -icanon     ## Turn off line buffering
printf "${ESC}[?${mv}h        "  ## Turn on mouse reporting
printf "${ESC}[?25l"  ## Turn off cursor

printat() #@ USAGE: printat ROW COLUMN
{
    printf "${ESC}[${1};${2}H"
}

print_buttons()
{
   num_but=$#
   gutter=2
   gutters=$(( $num_but + 1 ))
   but_width=$(( ($COLUMNS - $gutters) / $num_but ))
   n=0
   for but_str
   do
     col=$(( $gutter + $n * ($but_width + $gutter) ))
     printat $but_row $col
     printf "${ESC}[7m%${but_width}s" " "
     printat $but_row $(( $col + ($but_width - ${#but_str}) / 2 ))
     printf "%.${but_width}s${ESC}[0m" "$but_str"
     n=$(( $n + 1 ))
   done
}
```

```
clear
while :
do
  [ $mv -eq 9 ] && mv_str="Click to Show Press & Release" ||
                   mv_str="Click to Show Press Only"
  print_buttons "$mv_str" "Exit"

  read -n6 x

  m1=${x#????}    ## Remove the first 3 characters
  m2=${x#?????}   ## Remove the first 4 characters
  m3=${x#??????}  ## Remove the first 5 characters

  ## Convert to characters to decimal values
  printf -v mb "%d" "'$m1"
  printf -v mx "%d" "'$m2"
  printf -v my "%d" "'$m3"
  ## Values > 127 are signed
  [ $mx -lt 0 ] && MOUSEX=$(( 223 + $mx )) || MOUSEX=$(( $mx - 32 ))
  [ $my -lt 0 ] && MOUSEY=$(( 223 + $my )) || MOUSEY=$(( $my - 32 ))

  ## Button pressed is in first 2 bytes; use bitwise AND
  BUTTON=$(( ($mb & 3) + 1 ))

  case $MOUSEY in
      $but_row) ## Calculate which on-screen button has been pressed
                button=$(( ($MOUSEX - $gutter) / $but_width + 1 ))
                case $button in
                    1) printf "${ESC}[?${mv}l"
                       [ $mv -eq 9 ] && mv=1000 || mv=9
                       printf "${ESC}[?${mv}h"
                       [ $mv -eq 1000 ] && x=$(dd bs=1 count=6 2>/dev/null)
                       ;;
                    2) break ;;
                esac
                ;;
      *) printat $MOUSEY $MOUSEX
         printf "X=%d Y=%d [%d]  " $MOUSEX $MOUSEY $BUTTON
         ;;
  esac

done

printf "${ESC}[?${mv}l"  ## Turn off mouse reporting
stty "$_STTY"            ## Restore terminal settings
printf "${ESC}[?12l${ESC}[?25h" ## Turn cursor back on
printf "\n${ESC}[0J\n"   ## Clear from cursor to bottom of screen
```

Summary

Bash has a rich set of options for interactive programming. In this chapter, you learned how to leverage that to read any keystroke, including function keys and others that return more than a single character.

Exercises

1. Using the key-funcs library, write a menu script that uses the function keys for selection.

2. Rewrite the key-funcs library to include mouse handling, and incorporate the function into the mouse-demo script.

3. The password script does minimal checking for invalid entries. What checking would you add? How would you code it?

Shell Variables

This list is excerpted from the bash man page and edited to make a stand-alone document. The following variables are set by bash.

BASH

Expands to the full file name used to invoke this instance of bash.

BASHPID

Expands to the process ID of the current bash process. This differs from $$ under certain circumstances, such as subshells that do not require bash to be reinitialized.

BASH_ALIASES

An associative array variable whose members correspond to the internal list of aliases as maintained by the alias builtin. Elements added to this array appear in the alias list; unsetting array elements causes aliases to be removed from the alias list.

BASH_ARGC

An array variable whose values are the number of parameters in each frame of the current bash execution call stack. The number of parameters to the current subroutine (shell function or script executed with . or source) is at the top of the stack. When a subroutine is executed, the number of parameters passed is pushed onto BASH_ARGC. The shell sets BASH_ARGC only when in extended debugging mode (see the description of the extdebug option to the shopt builtin in the bash man page).

BASH_ARGV

An array variable containing all the parameters in the current bash execution call stack. The final parameter of the last subroutine call is at the top of the stack; the first parameter of the initial call is at the bottom. When a subroutine is executed, the parameters supplied are pushed onto BASH_ARGV. The shell sets BASH_ARGV only when in extended debugging mode (see the description of the extdebug option to the shopt builtin in the bash man page).

BASH_CMDS

An associative array variable whose members correspond to the internal hash table of commands as maintained by the hash builtin. Elements added to this array appear in the hash table; unsetting array elements causes commands to be removed from the hash table.

BASH_COMMAND

The command currently being executed or about to be executed, unless the shell is executing a command as the result of a trap, in which case it is the command executing at the time of the trap.

BASH_EXECUTION_STRING

The command argument to the -c invocation option.

BASH_LINENO

An array variable whose members are the line numbers in source files corresponding to each member of FUNCNAME. ${BASH_LINENO[$i]} is the line number in the source file where ${FUNCNAME[$i]} was called (or ${BASH_LINENO[$i-1]} if referenced within another shell function). The corresponding source file name is ${BASH_SOURCE[$i]}. Use LINENO to obtain the current line number.

BASH_REMATCH

An array variable whose members are assigned by the =~ binary operator to the [[conditional command. The element with index 0 is the portion of the string matching the entire regular expression. The element with index n is the portion of the string matching the nth parenthesized subexpression. This variable is read-only.

BASH_SOURCE

An array variable whose members are the source file names corresponding to the elements in the FUNCNAME array variable.

BASH_SUBSHELL

Incremented by one each time a subshell or subshell environment is spawned. The initial value is 0.

BASH_VERSINFO

A read-only array variable whose members hold version information for this instance of bash. The values assigned to the array members are as follows:

BASH_VERSINFO[0]: The major version number (the release)

BASH_VERSINFO[1]: The minor version number (the version)

BASH_VERSINFO[2]: The patch level

BASH_VERSINFO[3]: The build version

BASH_VERSINFO[4]: The release status (e.g., beta1)

BASH_VERSINFO[5]: The value of MACHTYPE

BASH_VERSION

Expands to a string describing the version of this instance of bash.

COMP_CWORD

An index into ${COMP_WORDS} of the word containing the current cursor position. This variable is available only in shell functions invoked by the programmable completion facilities (see "Programmable Completion" in the bash man page).

COMP_KEY

The key (or final key of a key sequence) used to invoke the current completion function.

COMP_LINE

The current command line. This variable is available only in shell functions and external commands invoked by the programmable completion facilities (see "Programmable Completion" in the bash man page).

COMP_POINT

The index of the current cursor position relative to the beginning of the current command. If the current cursor position is at the end of the current command, the value of this variable is equal to ${#COMP_LINE}. This variable is available only in shell functions and external commands invoked by the programmable completion facilities (see "Programmable Completion" in the bash man page).

COMP_TYPE

Set to an integer value corresponding to the type of completion attempted that caused a completion function to be called: TAB for normal completion, ? for listing completions after successive tabs, ! for listing alternatives on partial word completion, @ to list completions if the word is not unmodified, or % for menu completion. This variable is available only in shell functions and external commands invoked by the programmable completion facilities (see "Programmable Completion" in the bash man page).

COMP_WORDBREAKS

The set of characters that the readline library treats as word separators when performing word completion. If COMP_WORDBREAKS is unset, it loses its special properties, even if it is subsequently reset.

COMP_WORDS

An array variable (see "Arrays" in the bash man page) consisting of the individual words in the current command line. The line is split into words as readline would split it, using COMP_WORDBREAKS as described previously. This variable is available only in shell functions invoked by the programmable completion facilities (see "Programmable Completion" in the bash man page).

DIRSTACK

An array variable (see "Arrays" in the bash man page) containing the current contents of the directory stack. Directories appear in the stack in the order they are displayed by the dirs builtin. Assigning to members of this array variable may be used to modify directories already in the stack, but the pushd and popd builtins must be used to add and remove directories. Assignment to this variable will not change the current directory. If DIRSTACK is unset, it loses its special properties, even if it is subsequently reset.

EUID

Expands to the effective user ID of the current user, initialized at shell startup. This variable is read-only.

FUNCNAME

An array variable containing the names of all shell functions currently in the execution call stack. The element with index 0 is the name of any currently executing shell function. The bottom-most element is main. This variable exists only when a shell function is executing. Assignments to FUNCNAME have no effect and return an error status. If FUNCNAME is unset, it loses its special properties, even if it is subsequently reset.

GROUPS

An array variable containing the list of groups of which the current user is a member. Assignments to GROUPS have no effect and return an error status. If GROUPS is unset, it loses its special properties, even if it is subsequently reset.

HISTCMD

The history number, or index in the history list, of the current command. If HISTCMD is unset, it loses its special properties, even if it is subsequently reset.

HOSTNAME

Automatically set to the name of the current host.

HOSTTYPE

Automatically set to a string that uniquely describes the type of machine on which bash is executing. The default is system-dependent.

LINENO

Each time this parameter is referenced, the shell substitutes a decimal number representing the current sequential line number (starting with 1) within a script or function. When not in a script or function, the value substituted is not guaranteed to be meaningful. If LINENO is unset, it loses its special properties, even if it is subsequently reset.

MACHTYPE

Automatically set to a string that fully describes the system type on which bash is executing, in the standard GNU cpu-company-system format. The default is system-dependent.

OLDPWD

The previous working directory as set by the cd command.

OPTARG

The value of the last option argument processed by the getopts builtin command (see "Shell Builtin Commands" in the bash man page).

OPTIND

The index of the next argument to be processed by the getopts builtin command (see "Shell Builtin Commands" in the bash man page).

OSTYPE

Automatically set to a string that describes the operating system on which bash is executing. The default is system-dependent.

PIPESTATUS

An array variable (see "Arrays" in the bash man page) containing a list of exit status values from the processes in the most recently executed foreground pipeline (which may contain only a single command).

PPID

The process ID of the shell's parent. This variable is read-only.

PWD

The current working directory as set by the cd command.

RANDOM

Each time this parameter is referenced, a random integer between 0 and 32767 is generated. The sequence of random numbers may be initialized by assigning a value to RANDOM. If RANDOM is unset, it loses its special properties, even if it is subsequently reset.

REPLY

Set to the line of input read by the read builtin command when no arguments are supplied.

SECONDS

Each time this parameter is referenced, the number of seconds since shell invocation is returned. If a value is assigned to SECONDS, the value returned upon subsequent references is the number of seconds since the assignment plus the value assigned. If SECONDS is unset, it loses its special properties, even if it is subsequently reset.

SHELLOPTS

A colon-separated list of enabled shell options. Each word in the list is a valid argument for the -o option to the set builtin command (see "Shell Builtin Commands" in the bash man page). The options appearing in SHELLOPTS are those reported as on by set -o. If this variable is in the environment when bash starts up, each shell option in the list will be enabled before reading any startup files. This variable is read-only.

SHLVL

Incremented by one each time an instance of bash is started.

UID

Expands to the user ID of the current user, initialized at shell startup. This variable is read-only.

The following variables are used by the shell. In some cases, bash assigns a default value to a variable; these cases are noted in the following sections.

BASH_ENV

If this parameter is set when bash is executing a shell script, its value is interpreted as a file name containing commands to initialize the shell, as in ~/.bashrc. The value of BASH_ENV is subjected to parameter expansion, command substitution, and arithmetic expansion before being interpreted as a file name. PATH is not used to search for the resultant file name.

CDPATH

The search path for the cd command. This is a colon-separated list of directories in which the shell looks for destination directories specified by the cd command. A sample value is .:~:/usr.

COLUMNS

Used by the select builtin command to determine the terminal width when printing selection lists. This is automatically set upon receipt of a SIGWINCH.

COMPREPLY

An array variable from which bash reads the possible completions generated by a shell function invoked by the programmable completion facility (see "Programmable Completion" in the bash man page).

EMACS

If bash finds this variable in the environment when the shell starts with value t, it assumes that the shell is running in an emacs shell buffer and disables line editing.

FCEDIT

The default editor for the fc builtin command.

FIGNORE

A colon-separated list of suffixes to ignore when performing file name completion (see READLINE in the bash man page). A file name whose suffix matches one of the entries in FIGNORE is excluded from the list of matched file names. A sample value is .o:~.

GLOBIGNORE

A colon-separated list of patterns defining the set of file names to be ignored by pathname expansion. If a file name matched by a pathname expansion pattern also matches one of the patterns in GLOBIGNORE, it is removed from the list of matches.

HISTCONTROL

A colon-separated list of values controlling how commands are saved on the history list. If the list of values includes ignorespace, lines that begin with a space character are not saved in the history list. A value of ignoredups causes lines matching the previous history entry to not be saved. A value of ignoreboth is shorthand for ignorespace and ignoredups. A value of erasedups causes all previous lines matching the current line to be removed from the history list before that line is saved. Any value not in the previous list is ignored. If HISTCONTROL is unset or does not include a valid value, all lines read by the shell parser are saved on the history list, subject to the value of HISTIGNORE. The second and subsequent lines of a multiline compound command are not tested and are added to the history regardless of the value of HISTCONTROL.

HISTFILE

The name of the file in which command history is saved (see HISTORY in the bash man page). The default value is ~/.bash_history. If unset, the command history is not saved when an interactive shell exits.

HISTFILESIZE

The maximum number of lines contained in the history file. When this variable is assigned a value, the history file is truncated, if necessary, by removing the oldest entries to contain no more than that number of lines. The default value is 500. The history file is also truncated to this size after writing it when an interactive shell exits.

HISTIGNORE

A colon-separated list of patterns used to decide which command lines should be saved on the history list. Each pattern is anchored at the beginning of the line and must match the complete line (no implicit * is appended). Each pattern is tested against the line after the checks specified by HISTCONTROL are applied. In addition to the normal shell pattern matching characters, & matches the previous history line. & may be escaped using a backslash; the backslash is removed before attempting a match. The second and subsequent lines of a multiline compound command are not tested and are added to the history regardless of the value of HISTIGNORE.

HISTSIZE

The number of commands to remember in the command history (see HISTORY in the bash man page). The default value is 500.

HISTTIMEFORMAT

If this variable is set and not null, its value is used as a format string for strftime(3) to print the time stamp associated with each history entry displayed by the history builtin. If this variable is set, time stamps are written to the history file so they may be preserved across shell sessions. This uses the history comment character to distinguish timestamps from other history lines.

HOME

The home directory of the current user; the default argument for the cd builtin command. The value of this variable is also used when performing tilde expansion.

HOSTFILE

Contains the name of a file in the same format as /etc/hosts that should be read when the shell needs to complete a hostname. The list of possible hostname completions may be changed while the shell is running; the next time hostname completion is attempted after the value is changed, bash adds the contents of the new file to the existing list. If HOSTFILE is set but has no value, bash attempts to read /etc/hosts to obtain the list of possible hostname completions. When HOSTFILE is unset, the hostname list is cleared.

IFS

The Internal Field Separator that is used for word splitting after expansion and to split lines into words with the read builtin command. The default value is ' '.

IGNOREEOF

Controls the action of an interactive shell on receipt of an EOF character as the sole input. If set, the value is the number of consecutive EOF characters that must be typed as the first characters on an input line before bash exits. If the variable exists but does not have a numeric value or does not have a value, the default value is 10. If it does not exist, EOF signifies the end of input to the shell.

INPUTRC

The file name for the readline startup file, overriding the default of ~/.inputrc (see READLINE in the bash man page).

LANG

Used to determine the locale category for any category not specifically selected with a variable starting with LC_.

LC_ALL

This variable overrides the value of LANG and any other LC_ variable specifying a locale category.

LC_COLLATE

This variable determines the collation order used when sorting the results of pathname expansion and determines the behavior of range expressions, equivalence classes, and collating sequences within pathname expansion and pattern matching.

LC_CTYPE

This variable determines the interpretation of characters and the behavior of character classes within pathname expansion and pattern matching.

LC_MESSAGES

This variable determines the locale used to translate double-quoted strings preceded by a $.

LC_NUMERIC

This variable determines the locale category used for number formatting.

LINES

Used by the `select` builtin command to determine the column length for printing selection lists. This is automatically set upon receipt of a `SIGWINCH`.

MAIL

If this parameter is set to a file name and the `MAILPATH` variable is not set, `bash` informs the user of the arrival of mail in the specified file.

MAILCHECK

Specifies how often (in seconds) `bash` checks for mail. The default is 60 seconds. When it is time to check for mail, the shell does so before displaying the primary prompt. If this variable is unset or set to a value that is not a number greater than or equal to zero, the shell disables mail checking.

MAILPATH

A colon-separated list of file names to be checked for mail. The message to be printed when mail arrives in a particular file may be specified by separating the file name from the message with a ?. When used in the text of the message, $_ expands to the name of the current mail file. Here's an example:

```
MAILPATH='/var/mail/bfox?"You have mail":~/shell-mail?"$_ has mail!"'
```

Bash supplies a default value for this variable, but the location of the user mail files that it uses is system dependent (for example, `/var/mail/$USER`).

OPTERR

If set to the value 1, bash displays error messages generated by the getopts builtin command (see "Shell Builtin Commands" in the bash man page). OPTERR is initialized to 1 each time the shell is invoked or a shell script is executed.

PATH

The search path for commands. It is a colon-separated list of directories in which the shell looks for commands (see "Command Execution" in the bash man page). A zero-length (null) directory name in the value of PATH indicates the current directory. A null directory name may appear as two adjacent colons or as an initial or trailing colon. The default path is system-dependent and is set by the administrator who installs bash. A common value is /usr/gnu/bin:/usr/local/bin:/usr/ucb:/bin:/usr/bin.

POSIXLY_CORRECT

If this variable is in the environment when bash starts, the shell enters POSIX mode before reading the startup files, as if the --posix invocation option had been supplied. If it is set while the shell is running, bash enables POSIX mode, as if the command set -o posix had been executed.

PROMPT_COMMAND

If set, the value is executed as a command prior to issuing each primary prompt.

PROMPT_DIRTRIM

If set to a number greater than zero, the value is used as the number of trailing directory components to retain when expanding the \w and \W prompt string escapes (see "Prompting" in the bash man page). Characters removed are replaced with an ellipsis.

PS1

The value of this parameter is expanded (see "Prompting" in the bash man page) and used as the primary prompt string. The default value is "\s-\v\$ ".

PS2

The value of this parameter is expanded as with PS1 and used as the secondary prompt string. The default is "> ".

PS3

The value of this parameter is used as the prompt for the select command (see "SHELL GRAMMAR" earlier).

PS4

The value of this parameter is expanded as with PS1, and the value is printed before each command bash displays during an execution trace. The first character of PS4 is replicated multiple times, as necessary, to indicate multiple levels of indirection. The default is "+ ".

SHELL

The full pathname to the shell is kept in this environment variable. If it is not set when the shell starts, bash assigns to it the full pathname of the current user's login shell.

TIMEFORMAT

The value of this parameter is used as a format string specifying how the timing information for pipelines prefixed with the time reserved word should be displayed. The % character introduces an escape sequence that is expanded to a time value or other information. The escape sequences and their meanings are as follows; the braces denote optional portions.

%%: A literal %.

%[p][1]R: The elapsed time in seconds.

%[p][1]U: The number of CPU seconds spent in user mode.

%[p][1]S: The number of CPU seconds spent in system mode.

%P: The CPU percentage, computed as (%U + %S) / %R. The optional p is a digit specifying the precision, the number of fractional digits after a decimal point. A value of 0 causes no decimal point or fraction to be output. At most three places after the decimal point may be specified; values of p greater than 3 are changed to 3. If p is not specified, the value 3 is used. The optional l specifies a longer format, including minutes, of the form MMmSS.FFs. The value of p determines whether the fraction is included. If this variable is not set, bash acts as if it had the value

`$'\nreal\t%3lR\nuser\t%3lU\nsys%3lS'`. If the value is null, no timing information is displayed. A trailing newline is added when the format string is displayed.

TMOUT

If set to a value greater than zero, `TMOUT` is treated as the default timeout for the read builtin. The select command terminates if input does not arrive after `TMOUT` seconds when input is coming from a terminal. In an interactive shell, the value is interpreted as the number of seconds to wait for input after issuing the primary prompt. `Bash` terminates after waiting for that number of seconds if input does not arrive.

TMPDIR

If set, `bash` uses its value as the name of a directory in which `bash` creates temporary files for the shell's use.

auto_resume

This variable controls how the shell interacts with the user and job control. If this variable is set, single word simple commands without redirections are treated as candidates for resumption of an existing stopped job. There is no ambiguity allowed; if there is more than one job beginning with the string typed, the job most recently accessed is selected. The name of a stopped job, in this context, is the command line used to start it. If set to the value exact, the string supplied must match the name of a stopped job exactly; if set to substring, the string supplied needs to match a substring of the name of a stopped job. The substring value provides functionality analogous to the `%?` job identifier (see "Job Control" in the bash man page). If set to any other value, the supplied string must be a prefix of a stopped job's name; this provides functionality analogous to the `%string` job identifier.

histchars

The two or three characters that control history expansion and tokenization (see "History Expansion" in the bash man page). The first character is the history expansion character, the character that signals the start of a history expansion, normally !. The second character is the quick substitution character, which is used as shorthand for rerunning the previous command entered, substituting one string for another in the command. The default is ^. The optional third character is the character that indicates that the remainder of the line is a comment when found as the first character of a word, normally #. The history comment character causes history substitution to be skipped for the remaining words on the line. It does not necessarily cause the shell parser to treat the rest of the line as a comment.

Index

■Special Characters

!(pattern-list), 92
!= operator, 20
(hash), 5
#! (shebang), 5
$ (dollar sign), 33
$- parameter, 8
$! parameter, 8
$# parameter, 8, 53
$$ parameter, 8
$* parameter, 8
$? parameter, 8, 19
$@ parameter, 8, 29
$_ parameter, 8
$_KEY variable, 194
${!var} expansion, 52
${#var} expansion, 49
${var#PATTERN} expansion, 51
${var##PATTERN} expansion, 51
${var%PATTERN} expansion, 50, 70
${var%%PATTERN} expansion, 50
${var,PATTERN} expansion, 53
${var//PATTERN/STRING} expansion, 51
${var?message} expansion, 49
${var^PATTERN} expansion, 52
${var+alternate} expansion, 47–48
${var=default} expansion, 48
${var:?} expansion, 164
${var:?message} expansion, 49
${var:+alternate} expansion, 47–48
${var:=default} expansion, 48
${var\:-default} expansion, 47
${var:OFFSET:LENGTH} expansion, 51
${var-default} expansion, 47
$0 parameter, 8
% modulo operator, 33
%b specifier, 10

%d specifier, 11
%e specifier, 11
%f specifier, 11
%s specifier, 10, 181–182
%x specifier, 11
%X specifier, 11
&& operator, 19, 21, 23
((...)), 22
((reserved word, 19
* (asterisk), 37
* subscript, 54
*(pattern-list), 92
? (wildcard), 69
?(pattern-list), 92
\ (backslash), 8, 10, 13, 99
` (backtick), 16, 35
@ subscript, 54
@(pattern-list), 92
[[...]], 21
[[reserved word, 19
|| operator, 19, 21
+(pattern-list), 92
<(command), 37
= operator, 20
=~ operator, 21
== operator, 20
> redirection operator, 13
>(command), 37
>> operator, 14

■A

a function, 129
-a option, 21, 38, 100, 107
absolute pathnames, 2
agridsize variable, 169
alert function, 69, 78
alias command, 109

You Need the Companion eBook

Your purchase of this book entitles you to buy the companion PDF-version eBook for only $10. Take the weightless companion with you anywhere.

We believe this Apress title will prove so indispensable that you'll want to carry it with you everywhere, which is why we are offering the companion eBook (in PDF format) for $10 to customers who purchase this book now. Convenient and fully searchable, the PDF version of any content-rich, page-heavy Apress book makes a valuable addition to your programming library. You can easily find and copy code—or perform examples by quickly toggling between instructions and the application. Even simultaneously tackling a donut, diet soda, and complex code becomes simplified with hands-free eBooks!

Once you purchase your book, getting the $10 companion eBook is simple:

❶ Visit **www.apress.com/promo/tendollars/**.

❷ Complete a basic registration form to receive a randomly generated question about this title.

❸ Answer the question correctly in 60 seconds, and you will receive a promotional code to redeem for the $10.00 eBook.

THE EXPERT'S VOICE™

233 Spring Street, New York, NY 10013

Offer valid through 4/10.